The BEST Book of How to Behave Badly Ever!

THIS IS A CARLTON BOOK

Copyright © 1999 Carlton Books Ltd

First published in 1999
by Carlton Books Ltd
20 St Anne's Court
Wardour Street
London W1V 3AW

ISBN 1 85868 677 6

A CIP catalogue record for this book is available from the British Library

2 4 6 8 10 9 7 5 3 1

Printed and bound in Great Britain

The BEST Book of How to Behave Badly Ever!

EVERY MAN'S GUIDE to ANNOYING, AGGRAVATING and IRRITATING

H U W   J A R S Z

CARLTON

CONTENTS

Foreword

by Ivor Biggun

Despite the best efforts of Noel Edmonds, the ability to irritate people remains a sadly neglected art form. Through the caring, sharing Nineties and the birth of the 'New Man', there has been a real danger that men are becoming so obsessed with political correctness, doing the ironing and darning their own socks that they are forgetting the very essentials of male life – like getting bladdered, making tasteless remarks to the opposite sex, scratching scrotums (preferably their own) in public and farting in confined spaces. But fear not, help is at hand.

This book gives you many a pointer to how to *really* annoy others, so that people will regularly accuse you of ruining their day – at work, at a party, on holiday, in hospital, at a concert, in the supermarket or even on a golf course. So if you're sick of being polite and your idea of getting the most out of life is an extra portion of vindaloo for super trumpet farts in the morning, read on.

Just don't complain to me or Huw when you are avoided like a turd in a swimming pool, because all we'll say is "told you so."

Chapter One:

Time in a Bottle

A Potted History of Behaving Badly

323 BC: After defeating Greece, Persia (after a replay), Egypt and bits of present-day India, the all-conquering Alexander the Great celebrated victory too heartily one evening and dropped dead during a drinking contest at the age of 32.

AD 25: Roman Emperor Tiberius invented a great game for livening up the dullest of parties. He would force a guest to drink so much wine that his bladder would be in danger of overflowing. Then just as the guest was fit to burst and was absolutely desperate for a piss, Tiberius would tie up the poor man's genitals with a lute string. It never failed to make the party go with a swing.

48: Claudius was more of a killjoy when it came to parties. He went off them after discovering that his wife, Messalina, was a bit of an old slapper who used to put it about at parties. So he had her executed along with 300 guests. At least it improved his chances of winning the next game.

69: Roman Emperor Vitellius loved his food so much that he invariably used to go back for seconds. The reason he always had room for more was that between courses he would stick a feather down his throat and disgorge what he'd just eaten. Nobody queued up to sit next to him at the dinner table.

211: Young Roman emperor Heliogabalus had a pair of dinner guests suffocated in rose petals for the sheer hell of it.

334: Chinese Emperor Shih Hu was a firm believer in fresh meat – especially human. Whereas other rulers might select a chicken or a pig to be slaughtered, Shih Hu selected the dish of the day from his own harem. He would pick a girl, have her beheaded and then have the body served as the main course. If any girl protested however, she was likely to be spared. After all, he didn't want to eat anything that disagreed with him.

453: Attila the Hun, another guy who was always the life and soul of the party, had the misfortune to pop his clogs on his 12th honeymoon after a particularly energetic shag. Still, what a way to go...

707: Pope John VII was bludgeoned to death by an irate husband who discovered His Holiness on top of his wife. Some people have no sense of humour.

955: Pope John XII was not averse to a spot of rumpty-tumpty and turned the papal palace into a brothel, which isn't really in keeping with the spirit of the post.

1032: Pope Benedict IX was another promiscuous pontiff. He was into bisexuality, bestiality, witchcraft and

Satanism, none of which prevented him serving three terms in office. He ended up selling the papacy to his godfather.

1206: Genghis Khan conquered Mongolia which was a bit of a waste of time really since there's nothing much there – no decent pubs, no beaches, not even a branch of Ikea. But he had fun along the way, and anyway, he eventually managed to stretch his empire right across Asia to the Black Sea. He was very much Asia's main man. If you needed tickets for the Mongolia Camel Derby or to see Ulan Bator's answer to the Brotherhood of Man, Genghis was *the* guy. The only trouble was he was just as likely to disembowel you as give you the time of day. As Geoffrey Boycott would say: he was big on disembowelling, was Genghis. Indeed it would probably have been his specialist subject on *Mastermind*. But he did have a more sensitive side. Once he was about to have an enemy executed when he realised that the man was an old childhood friend. So Genghis ordered that the execution be cancelled and instead had the man rolled in a carpet and kicked to death. See, he was just a big softie really.

1135: Henry I, King of England pegged out after pigging out on lampreys (small eel-like creatures) at a banquet in France.

1193: Philip II Augustus, King of France, decided half-way through his wedding ceremony that he didn't really fancy his Danish bride Ingeborg after all. Why should it always be a woman's prerogative to change her mind, he thought? Besides, he was King so he could do what he wanted. So at the end of the reception, when all the speeches were over, the last of the prawn vol-au-vents had gone and the best man had been sick over one of the bridesmaids, Philip had Ingeborg locked away, first in a nunnery and then in various prisons. And there she remained for years while Phil carried on with some German floosie.

1216: King John went to meet his maker after tucking into too many peaches and vast quantites of cider – always an inadvisable mix. Not only did he not live to see the effects of Magna Carta, but he missed out on a fortune in royalties from the Robin Hood story.

1327: Roger Mortimer was a rather unscrupulous character – not the sort you'd want to bump into down a dark alley. In fact he was something of an expert on back passages and earned his place in history by murdering Edward II in quite spectacular fashion. While two accomplices held the king down, Mortimer rammed a long, open-topped deer's horn up the royal rectum. With this in position, Mortimer inserted the red-hot tip of a long-handled poker through the horn and deep into Edward's bowels. Since there were no visible marks on the body, death was put down to natural causes.

1383: Tamburlaine was a descendant of Genghis Khan and inherited many of his less savoury character traits. On one occasion he had 5,000 people beheaded and proceeded to use their heads to build a pyramid. It was also said that anyone who attempted to crack a joke in his presence was immediately put to death, making it a tragedy that Freddie Starr's act never took him to Mongolia.

1399: Henry IV became King of England and adopted the skinhead look mainly because he had so many head lice that his hair wouldn't grow. This was despite frequent applications of his favourite shampoo, Wash 'n' Crawl.

1465: Vlad the Impaler had 20,000 of his enemies impaled on wooden stakes, thereby inventing the kebab. To wash it down, he liked to drink the blood of his victims and forced women to eat the cooked flesh of their husbands. He was also quite fond of persuading parents to eat their children. When a delegation of somewhat optimistic Turkish envoys turned up on a peace mission, he had their hats and coats nailed to their bodies. He was subsequently re-christened Vlad the Lad.

1536: Henry VIII had his second wife Anne Boleyn beheaded for messing around. Six years later, he repeated the trick with his fifth wife, Catherine Howard. Any bloke who can land six wives and wield his mighty chopper on two of them can't be all bad. Anyway he deserved a medal for putting up with the pig-ugly Anne of Cleves for six months.

1544: Pope Paul III had something like 45,000 prostitutes on his payroll, making him probably the world's most successful pimp.

1561: Don Carlos, son of Phillip II of Spain, was so dissatisfied with a pair of boots made specially for him that he hacked them into pieces and forced the cobbler to eat them. He later got a job on the customer complaints counter with Dolcis.

1584: Russian Czar Ivan the Terrible lived up to his name by indulging in such rumbustious foreplay that he killed his third wife before he'd even got his full ration of oats. He had his seventh wife drowned after he found she had been telling him porkies about claiming to be a virgin and had his sixth wife's lover impaled on a stake beneath her bedroom window. All in all, not the sort of husband you'd want to catch you with your trousers round your ankles within a 100-mile radius of his wife. He also enjoyed inventing particularly barbaric means of death. He had one enemy roasted alive on a spit and arranged for the treacherous Archbishop of Novgorod to be sewn into a bearskin and hunted down by a pack of hounds. That's one they haven't tried on *You Bet!* Boringly, for one who led such a colourful life, he died playing chess. Perhaps he was trying to behead the bishop.

1595: To obtain a clear run at the throne, Turkish sultan Mahomet III had all his 19 brothers murdered. Away from the pleasures of mass homicide, his hobbies included torturing women for hours on end. Not the kind of guy you'd want to be on the wrong side of.

1603: His lofty status was just about the only reason James I was invited to dinner parties. For his tongue was so big for his mouth that he used to slobber his food and drink all over the table. He also had a fondness for picking his nose in public and for never discarding old clothes. Whenever he wore a hole in his trousers, he didn't chuck them out or take them off but slipped another pair on top instead. By the end of his reign, he must have looked like Pavarotti. James is usually portrayed as a dour Scot in the 'Kenny Dalglish mould', but in truth he was a bit of a practical joker. His favourite jape was sticking a live frog down the Earl of Pembroke's neck. The Earl topped it, however, by placing a pig in the King's bedroom. What larks!

1623: Turkish ruler Murad IV was particularly intolerant of smoking. Rather than waste time and money putting up signs or distributing leaflets, he found that a more effective way of getting across the message that smoking can seriously damage your health was to have anybody caught puffing away executed on the spot. He would then leave the bodies lying around the street as a warning to anyone else who might be tempted to light up. In fact, Murad was intolerant of just about anything, from drinking coffee after the hours of darkness, humming Persian tunes to generally having a good time. He once had a party of female picnickers drowned because they were making too much noise. If only he'd been around when St. Winifred's School Choir were on *Top of the Pops*.

1643: Louis XIV hated washing so much that he took only three baths in his 77-year life. The French have followed his example ever since.

1648: The accession of Mahomet IV as Turkish ruler. Long before Glenn Hoddle had the idea, Mahomet decided to keep a diary of his reign and employed a scribe named Abdi to act as his David Davies. At the end of one singularly uneventful day, Mahomet asked Abdi what he had written for that day's entry, to which the ghost writer replied 'zilch', or the Turkish equivalent. At this, Mahomet picked up a spear and impaled Abdi with it, telling him: 'Now you have something to write about.'

1686: Louis XIV certainly knew how to impress the fairer sex. His chosen method of telling his sister-in-law, the Duchess of Orleans, that she was a bit of a babe was to fart loudly in her presence. If only all women were that easy to pull...

1690: Prince Antoine I of Monaco took exception to the fact that his wife, Marie de Lorraine, had more lovers than Keith Floyd has had hot dinners. So he constructed straw effigies of them which he proceeded to hang in the palace courtyard. Every time Marie went anywhere, she was forced to pass beneath the effigies and was thus reminded her of her infidelity.

1697: Augustus II became King of Poland and embarked on a full-time career as a love machine, fathering 366 children (more than one for each day of the year), of which only one was legitimate. Since he had virtually sired an entire generation, it was only to be expected that he'd end up having the odd incestuous relationship along the way. This may sound an idyllic lifestyle, but remember, it must have cost him a fortune in birthday presents.

1700: Peter the Great, discovering that his wife Catherine had been enjoying a bit on the side, had the head of her lover chopped off and pickled in a jar which he then put on her bedside table... as a gentle reminder.

1712: Peter the Great's son, Alexis, maintained the family tradition of behaving badly by crapping in his bedroom and wiping his arse on the curtains, just before his wedding day. The moral is: never go on a Russian stag night.

1714: Whilst King George I of England was something of a babe magnet, he despised his wife Dorothea's pulling power. So naturally enough he had her imprisoned and when he learned that she had finally died, he celebrated by going out to the theatre.

1721: The ageing Duke of Orleans defied medical advice and took a mistress nearly 30 years his junior. The strain proved too much and he was found slumped in the fireplace from a stroke – by the smile on his face, more than one.

1725: The birth of Casanova, the original Italian stallion. Blessed with a voracious sexual appetite, Giovanni Jacopo Casanova set about sowing more seeds than Alan Titchmarsh. Inevitably this created the odd moment of confusion, such as when he fell for a bit of skirt named Leonilda. The old smoothie was so smitten that he asked for her hand in marriage, but when Leonilda's mother was introduced to her future son-in-law, she screamed and fainted. It turned out that she was one of Casanova's many ex-lovers who had borne his child 17 years earlier. So Casanova had been about to marry his own daughter. Even in 18th century Italy, this was frowned upon unless, of course, you had a note from your mum.

1740: Frederick the Great became King of Prussia. In many respects a fine statesman and a courageous soldier, he was also a keen dog fancier. Unfortunately he fancied them a little too much, especially his pet whippet bitches to whom he was said to have become romantically attached. No doubt they were quick out of the traps when Frederick was approaching.

1750: The death of John V of Portugal, a monarch who reputedly satisfied his twin passions for Catholicism and sex by bedding nuns. Nice work if you can get it.

1760: George II, filled with all those German sausages, farted so vigorously that he fell off the toilet and smashed his head fatally on a cabinet, thus bringing a new meaning to the phrase 'died on the throne'.

1795: It is fair to say that the future George IV was none too smitten with his bride-to-be, Princess Caroline of Brunswick. The only way he could go through with the wedding ceremony was to get blind drunk and even then he tried to escape half-way through the ceremony, only to be held in place by his father, mad King George III. When asked by the archbishop if there was any known impediment to the marriage, the groom started to cry. Not surprisingly, his visit to the marital bed that night was a brief one and he ended up falling asleep in the fireplace. Things didn't get any better and George offered Caroline £50,000 a year to stay out of Britain, but she refused. When Napoleon died, a messenger brought the news to George with the words: 'Congratulations, sire, your greatest enemy is dead.' 'Is she really?' replied George. The messenger shook his head. Caroline had another three months to go.

1806: Every day, British Prime Minister William Pitt the Younger used to knock back six bottles of port, two bottles of madeira and a bottle and a half of claret. He was often splendidly drunk in the Commons and would regularly disappear behind the Speaker's chair in mid-debate to throw up.

1830: Shropshire squire Jack Mytton scared the pants off his guests by riding a bear into the dining-room. He later developed a nasty bout of hiccups and tried to get rid of them by setting fire to his own night-shirt. Although sustaining severe burns, he did manage to cure the hiccups. So that's all right then.

1834: Lord Melbourne became Prime Minister. John Major he wasn't, since he was more interested in flagellation than cricket and probably got a veritable stiffy at the mere mention of Government whips.

1849: William Charles Macready was a giant of the English stage and an actor who knew just how to treat extras. When playing Shylock in *The Merchant of Venice*, he enlisted the services of an ageing thespian purely so that Macready could beat him up in the wings before each performance, just to get him in the mood. One day, the old man failed to show – he was probably in intensive care after the previous night's pummelling – and Macready was beside himself with anger. It so happened that a fan of Macready's appeared in the wings but before he could say what an honour it was to meet the great man, Macready had hurled him against a wall and beaten him black and blue.

1852: The Duke of Wellington proved that he could still make his soldier stand to attention at the age of 83 as he embarked on yet another affair. Throughout his married life, he had a string of mistresses as women found him irresistible. It must have been the boots.

1857: The birth of celebrated French farteur Le Petomane. As a child, Joseph Pujol swam in the sea near Marseilles where he practised holding his breath and diving deep. One day he felt a rush of icy cold water enter his bowels and rush up inside his intestines.

Next thing, wouldn't you know it, the water flooded out of him all over the beach. Just the sort of thing to put you off your '99'. Anyway when he joined the army, he told his fellow soldiers about his party piece. Naturally they thought it sounded a touch more interesting than the bloke who could recite every station on the Paris Metro and so they demanded a demonstration. By flexing his anal and abdominal muscles, he could shoot a jet of water five yards. He then moved on to air instead of water and the grand fart was born. In view of the fact that Maurice Chevalier was able to become a giant of the French entertainment industry just by singing in broken English and the Singing Nun was a rock sensation in the land of the beret (OK, so she's Belgian), it follows that anyone who could fart to order would become a true French megastar. So Pujol worked the routine into his new music-hall act, changed his name to Le Petomane ('the manic farter') and became the highest-paid act in France. Kneeling with his backside facing the audience, he was able to imitate everything from a little girl's delicate fart to a long slide depicting his mother-in-law. He did machine guns, cannon, thunder, the hooting of an owl, a swarm of bees, a pig and the odd musical opus. A particular favourite was "By The Light Of The Silvery Moon" which he achieved by inserting a small flute in his rectum, and he rarely hit a bum note. At the end of his 90-minute performance, he invited the audience to fart along with him, a bit like the finale in *Crackerjack*. Theatres were forced to hire nurses for his shows as women in tight corsets tended to pass out during his act – but as a result of laughing rather than the smell. After bringing pleasure to millions and doubling the sales of baked beans, he died in 1945.

1863: Prime Minister Viscount Palmerston was cited as co-respondent in a divorce case at the ripe old age of 79. A few years earlier he had tried his luck with one of Queen Victoria's ladies-in-waiting on a visit to Windsor Castle. His excuse was that he was out of his skull on port and had gone to the wrong bedroom. We've all tried that one! Still at least he had the good sense not to wave his todger about in front of Her Maj. Palmerston died from a heart attack while getting a slip of a parlour maid to chalk his cue on his private billiard table.

1886: Otto, younger brother of mad King Ludwig II of Bavaria, proved to be every bit as barking. Somewhat belatedly, he decided the only way to stay sane was to shoot a peasant every morning. Adhering to the old Bavarian saying, 'a peasant a day keeps the doctor away' (known thereafter as the Otto motto), he proceeded to take pot shots at those working in the royal garden. Fortunately his staff had taken the precaution of loading his gun with blank cartridges. As if Otto didn't have enough problems without his pistol firing blanks...

1888: U.S. President Grover Cleveland was accused of bestiality and frequenting brothels, two policies which have proved to be vote-winners with the American public ever since.

1896: Yorkshire cricketer Bobby Peel liked a jar or six before a match. More than once he drank himself into a condition which the cricketers' bible, *Wisden*, described as 'having to go away'. On one occasion he was suspended from the team by his captain for 'running the wrong way, and bowling at the pavilion in the belief that it was a batsman.' With all those white sweaters batsmen wear, it was an easy mistake to make. Matters came to a head, however, when a heavy night's drinking saw him take to the field the following morning and promptly empty his bladder all over the pitch. Peel was sacked but the moisture in the wicket went on to help the Yorkshire seamers.

1899: French President Felix Faure became a stiff while having sex in a Paris brothel. Faure's death came as such a shock to the woman (he hadn't even paid) that his todger had to be surgically removed from her. Still, he didn't feel a thing.

1901: As well as chasing anything in a corset, Edward VII was a renowned practical joker. He once put a dead seagull in a friend's bed and used to enjoy stubbing out lighted cigars on the backs of friends' hands. You had to laugh.

1916: Who said the Welsh don't know how to enjoy themselves? Prime Minister David Lloyd George managed to keep two women on the boil for ages – his wife and his secretary. And for good measure, he also bedded his daughter's governess. Small wonder that when his son answered a phone call asking whether the mistress of the house was available, he replied: 'Which one?'

1919: Fifty-four-year-old U.S. President Warren G. Harding did his bit for the youth of America by getting his schoolgirl mistress pregnant. This was the climax to a life of debauchery for Harding who usually passed his young lover, Nan Britton, off as his niece to avoid awkward questions. Besides Britton and one other long-term mistress, Harding regularly attended drunken orgies with chorus girls. No wonder every American politician wants to be President.

1921: Mao Tse-tung started up the Chinese Communist Party and decided never to take a bath or brush his teeth – the latter on the grounds that tigers never brushed their teeth either. Which is a bit like saying you're not going to buy your girlfriend a Christmas present because you never see a Thomson's gazelle in John Lewis's. But, despite his shortcomings in the hygiene department, Mao was no fool and, in his later years, he had a posse of young concubines on hand to rub him down with hot towels. Could be worth skipping a few baths in the hope of achieving similar results.

1936: The death of George V of England. He used to have a pet parrot which he would invite down for breakfast, much to the disgust of the Queen. As the bird wandered across the table, crapping to its heart's content, George had to keep moving the mustard pot and the sugar bowl to hide the droppings from his wife's eagle eye.

1969: Jim Morrison, lead singer with The Doors, was what being a rock star is all about. When he wasn't being arrested for being out of his skull, he was getting his todger out on stage. If Bobby Crush had whipped it out and flopped it on F sharp while in concert at the Buxton Tea Rooms, he too would have gone down in rock history.

1971: Another rock icon, Black Sabbath front-man Ozzy Osbourne, was said to have bitten off a bat's head on stage. It would have been a particularly desperate groupie who went for a snog with him after that. No tongues, surely.

1972: A Mr. Darsun Yilmaz from Damali on the Black Sea was so distraught after being rejected by his neighbour's daughter that he decided to kidnap her. Climbing a ladder to her room, he threw a blanket over the head of the sleeping figure in the bed and carried her downstairs to his waiting car. After whispering sweet nothings into her ear and telling her all the things he wanted to do to her, he pulled back the blanket to find instead that it contained his beloved's 91-year-old granny. She wasted no time in beating him soundly around the head.

1977: Elvis ate his last triple burger and large fries, washed down with a jumbo slice of chocolate cake. His death fuelled rumours that he'd only stayed loyal to Colonel Parker because he thought he owned the Kentucky Fried Chicken chain.

1978: Tom Horsley, a 30-year-old accountant from San José, California, didn't take too kindly to being stood up one evening. So he decided to sue his absent date, waitress Alyn Chesselet, on the grounds that she had 'broken an oral contract to have dinner and see the musical *The Wiz*.' He promptly put in a claim for £21 – to cover his mileage to and from San Francisco (at the standard rate of 9.4p a mile) and his time as a certified public accountant (at £4.70 per hour). When informed of his action, Miss Chesselet described Mr. Horsley as 'nuts'. It is not thought that they arranged to meet again.

1978: The death of Keith Moon, wild man drummer with The Who, who specialized in trashing hotel rooms and driving Rolls-Royces into swimming pools. He was also chastised on *Points of View* for wiping his nose on the sleeve of his leather jacket during a performance on Top of the Pops. Tut tut. By an uncanny coincidence, Moon died from an accidental overdose in the same London flat where 'Mama' Cass Elliot of the Mamas and Papas had choked to death on a sandwich four years earlier. And he didn't even have time to sweep up the crumbs.

1985: Having been left by his wife of eight years, spurned husband Donald Niblett took a bulldozer from his workplace and began demolishing the family house. Although neighbours called the police before the entire building was reduced to rubble, he still managed to cause £15,000 of damage.

1987: Holier-than-thou Assemblies of God minister Jimmy Swaggart was exposed for meeting New Orleans prostitute Debra Murphree at a New Orleans motel. It emerged that Swaggart, who had fiercely denounced other ministers' indiscretions from the pulpit, had been meeting Murphree for a year. She said that they never had sex but instead he preferred her to pose naked for him and talk about 'perverted' subjects.

1992: Clive Richley was stopped by police for driving his Reliant Robin at 104 mph on the M20 in Kent.

1994: One Milton Ross was sacked from his desk job at St. Joseph, Montana, for pissing into the office coffee pot. The misdemeanour was caught on video by his colleagues who had set up a camera after sensing that the water in their morning coffee seemed a bit off. It was a good job nobody asked for a milky one.

1995: Hugh Grant's career was temporarily put on hold following a spot of "Divine" intervention.

1996: California hairdresser Joseph Middleton was sentenced to 60-days' community service after tossing himself off with his free hand while doing a customer's hair with the other. He managed to finish both jobs to his satisfaction since the lady customer had been too scared to complain. She was probably just grateful she didn't go in for the blow dry.

1998: Bill Clinton. If only he'd paid to have Monica's dress dry-cleaned...

Chapter Two:

Situations

Two pints of lager and a packet of crisps please

IN THE PUB

The world is full of pointless proverbs. 'A stitch in time saves nine.' What's that all about then? Or: 'A nod's as good as a wink to a blind horse.' And what about: 'Too many cooks spoil the broth'. When was the last time you saw anybody making broth? There's certainly nothing wrong with the words 'bird' and 'bush' being used in conjunction with each other, but 'A bird in the hand is worth two in the bush' makes about as much sense as the Turkish entry for last year's Eurovision Song Contest. As for phrases like 'not saying boo to a goose', it would be far more relevant if it was not saying no to a goose. However there is one saying which most lads abide by: 'There is no such thing as a bad pub.' True, there are degrees of excellence – some pubs are markedly less wonderful than others – but unless there is a brewery strike or a sudden worldwide crisp famine, every pub has at least one redeeming feature.

What constitutes a good pub?

- Pumps which dispense every brand of lager known to man.

- Rows and rows of bottled lagers, including some specialist number brewed by an Albanian goatherd and his wife.

- No real ales, so you don't get loads of blokes in beards and Arran sweaters blocking the bar whilst they earnestly compare the relative merits of Widdlington's Old Knob and Grizzled Stoat. Just get it down your throat!

- Sexy barmaids in micro skirts (preferably female barmaids, preferably leather skirts) who aren't bright enough to cotton on to why everyone orders a bottle off the bottom shelf. The trick here is to stagger your order, buying nuts and crisps a packet at a time, as long as they are kept in a box on the floor so that she has to bend over. The resultant view is better than anything you get from Judith Chalmers on *Wish You Here Here?*

- A happy hour that lasts all day.

- A landlord who thinks lock-ins are a really good idea.

- A decent jukebox with a range of contemporary classics and plenty of blasts from the past to induce those mellow moments of nostalgia. After eight pints, you don't need Peggy Spencer to teach you the dance steps to Mud's "Tiger Feet".

- Somewhere situated next door to a modelling agency.

- At least one pool table and a darts board.

- A stripper every night of the week.

What constitutes a not-quite-so-good pub?

- One brand of pissy lager and some over-priced American

rubbish with the claim that it was the favourite tipple of Spiro T. Agnew and the bloke with the silly high-pitched voice out of The Stylistics.

- A place where they do hot meals all evening and have no separate eating areas. When you're downing pints at a steady rate, the only food you want to whiff is salt and vinegar, cheese and onion or smoky bacon crisps. You certainly don't want to find yourself stuck next to some gannet tucking into a plate full of shepherd's pie or roast chicken with Brussels sprouts.

- No barmaids, just lots of eager-to-please young men in poncy shirts. Alternatively, one geriatric barmaid whose legs look like a map of rivers of the world and who takes an eternity to serve you. Keep sending her back for something else in the hope that she'll expire beneath the optics and be replaced by a younger model.

- A happy hour for cocktails only.

- A landlord who calls last orders on time.

- No jukebox, just "Sounds Like Bert Kaempfert" playing.

- Somewhere situated next door to a Royal Mail sorting office (so you get lots of sweaty postmen coming in at the end of their rounds), an abattoir, sheltered accommodation or the head office of a feminist publishing company.

- No pub games, just an ancient pack of cards with the six of clubs missing.

- The only live entertainment is a jazz trio once a month. They play all the jazz greats (a contradiction in terms on a par with 'military intelligence' and 'fun run') and have a drummer who, instead of giving it some wellie like Keith Moon or even dear old Ringo (bless him), has one of those daft pastry brush things with which he caresses the cymbals. And they usually plonk themselves in a position so that nobody can get to the bog.

Pubs afford wonderful opportunities for behaving badly, both voluntary and involuntary. By its very nature, lager prompts certain bodily sounds which, when harnessed imaginatively, can be used as the basis for entertainment. A particular favourite is 'Fart the Intro' whereby each player has to pass wind to the tune of the introduction to a well-known song. As the evening progresses, this game becomes easier and easier to play with players holding it in for as long as possible before unleashing a veritable anal musical extravaganza. "Satisfaction" by the Stones is a good one for beginners – short and sharp – while things like "Remember You're a Womble" or 10cc's "Rubber Bullets" (both fast and furious) are strictly for experts or the incontinent. Since this is very much a spontaneous pastime, there should be no strict order of play. Anyone who has something to contribute should be allowed to do so the moment they are ready. Should there be an unfortunate loss of bowel control, resulting in the emission of something other than wind, that player will be disqualified and obliged to move elsewhere – at the very least, to sit on a stool.

Another popular pub pursuit is 'The Rowing Game', a classic drinking contest ideally staged where and when there is plenty of room. As with so many things in life, a lock-in is the perfect setting. Two teams sit down in rows on the floor as if they are boat race crews (but resist the temptation to kiss the cox of your crew). Each crew member has a full pint in his hand and, on the word 'Go!', the first player in each team downs the pint as swiftly as possible and turns the empty glass upside down on his head. Only then can the second member of the team start guzzling and so on until you reach the end. The winning team is the first to have all its members with upturned glasses on their heads. In their haste to win, some people will inevitably try and cut corners and end up with a lager shampoo. This game can become very competitive and rowdy, so it is probably best not to play it if the Round Table are holding a meeting in the corner or if there are more than two members of the local CID at the bar.

You will find that you can get away with a lot of things in pubs by the merest mention of the word 'traditional'. If an activity acquires the adjective 'traditional', it simultaneously gains a sudden respectability. No doubt when the Vikings invaded, they convinced the locals that rape and pillage were traditional. Similarly if your pub gets a new landlord – someone who is unfamiliar with the region – you can always try and persuade him that lock-ins, humping his barmaid over the counter, free drinks whenever there is a full moon, are all long-standing traditions in that neck of the woods. On a less ambitious scale, you can go for the 'Yard of Ale' – that 'traditional' drinking contest. Unless you want to spend the rest of the night emptying your bladder, it is best to make sure that the contents aren't exactly ale, but something more to your taste. Lager perhaps? A yard of advocaat is definitely not recommended unless the landlord is happy for half the pub to throw up and for his floor to resemble a sea of custard. The key to a successful Yard of Ale contest is to have a prize worth winning at the end of it all.

Prizes worth winning:

- Two weeks in Mauritius with Ulrika Jonsson.

- Free lager for a year.

- A new Ferrari.

- A French kiss from the barmaid.

- Brothel discount vouchers (valid in Amsterdam)

Prizes not worth winning:

- Two weeks in Walsall with Stan Collymore.

- A weekend at a monastery.

- As many pork scratchings as you can eat.

- A French kiss from the landlord.

- An embroidery set.

If one of the former are up for grabs, you may choose to indulge in a spot of sharp practice or, as those in the trade call it, cheating. There are three basic categories of cheating in a Yard of Ale contest – physical, verbal or tampering. Physical involves putting a rival competitor off by means of a subtle nudge in the ribs as he is half-way through the task, causing him to abort the mission and splutter liquid all over the table. In extreme cases, he may choke to death. Verbal intimidation during the challenge may take the form of a sudden shriek of horror; telling a joke, the punchline of which is so hilarious that the drinker will be too helpless with mirth to continue; or casually mentioning (within earshot of the contestant) the presence of a birthmark on the upper part of his girlfriend's thigh – information which he thought he alone was privy to. The effect will be instant and spectacular although it may also necessitate the summoning of paramedics. But if you reckon a night in casualty is a small price to pay for winning the contest, this is clearly the course of action for you. Tampering should be carried out beforehand. As the lager comes to a nice frothy head, nobody will notice the addition of a little squirt of Fairy Liquid cunningly concealed in your hand. And even if your opponent does manage to drink the entire yard in one go, the chances are that he will be foaming at the mouth to such an extent that he will have been put down by the RSPCA well before he has a chance to claim his prize.

19 WAYS TO UPSET MINE HOST

1. Sleep with the landlord's wife.
2. Sleep with the landlord's daughter.
3. Sleep with the landlord's wife and daughter.
4. Wake up with the hangover to end all hangovers to find yourself in bed with the landlord. *Note:* in some pubs this could earn you free lager for a year and two tickets for a George Michael concert.
5. Perform unnatural acts with the landlord's Ford Capri.
6. Switch over the football on the pub telly for *Gardeners' World.*
7. Win the jackpot regularly on the fruit machine.
8. Complain about his prices.

9. Roll around wild-eyed in agony on the floor after eating one of the 'pub grub' pork pies, only snatching breath to utter the words 'botulism' and 'compensation'. When the paramedics arrive to treat the landlord's coronary, tell him it was just a joke.

10. For an 80s night, invite a load of relatives who are in their eighties.

11. Belch loudly during the turn's tender Celine Dion ballad.

12. Set all the pub quiz questions on nuclear physics.

13. Lob peanuts down the barmaid's top (unless she is built like Mandy Dingle off *Emmerdale* or has big brothers).

14. Return from the loo and wave a condom under the barmaid's nose, even if you are on a promise.

15. Perform an unabridged version of *Riverdance* on a table.

16. Bleed copiously over the newly fitted dralon suite.

17. Re-enact Erika Roe's Twickenham streak across the bar.

18. Throw up over the brewery inspector.

19. In a pub full of bikers, put ten Roger Whittaker tracks on the jukebox, then exit sharply stage left.

How to Get Out of Buying a Round

In an era where people seem to be given awards for just about anything – Most Charismatic Accountant, Most Popular Member of the Inland Revenue, Best Supporting Bra Manufacturer, Most Promising Fortune Teller – it is surely an oversight that nobody has yet recognized the art of freeloading. Despite royal patronage, freeloading has no awards ceremony of its own and remains largely the preserve of councillors, MPs and young offenders. The best way to spot a freeloader is if his or her job title finishes with the word 'consultant' and their mission contains the words 'fact finding'. Over the years, some people have tended to confuse freeloaders and freemasons, but with freeloaders the greeting is made with the hand held out, palm up.

Given that the chances of a two-week fact-finding trip to Benidorm coming your way are slim, your best opportunity of entering into some serious freeloading is down at the pub. Obviously the first rule of successful freeloading is: always leave your wallet at home. However, it is advisable to secrete a small amount of change about your person – sufficient to buy yourself a couple of pints – just in case nobody takes the bait. This has the added advantage of convincing those about to buy you a drink that you are not entirely destitute. There are various reasons you can use to explain why you have forgotten your wallet:

- You had to leave your jeans at someone else's house when her husband returned home unexpectedly.

- You were mugged on the way to the pub. This is extremely useful for gaining the sympathy drink.

- The dog ate all your five and ten pound notes.

- Your girlfriend ate your credit cards.

- You left your wallet in your other jacket.

- You gave your last folding money to a Salvation Army collector.

- You felt in a charitable mood and bought 50 copies of The Big Issue on the way to the pub. They were too heavy to bring in.

- South Moluccan terrorists, armed with machine guns, burst into your home, kidnapped your girlfriend and demanded a ransom of £25. You had to pay up.

- Your girlfriend put your trousers with the money in the pocket in the automatic washing machine on hot cotton wash. All the notes are now in soggy shreds and the queen's head is imprinted on your underpants.

- Your house was destroyed by an Exocet missile during Neighbours.

An important thing to remember when trying to get out of buying a round is, never get too near to the bar. If you are in a group of half a dozen or more, always hover towards the back. Sooner or later, one of the group will seize the initiative and order the drinks before you all die of thirst. Then when glasses are emptying ready for the next round, suddenly announce that you're bursting for the loo, reminding everyone on the way out that yours is another pint. This can be repeated over and over so that you will be the last one due to buy a round. When it does come to your turn, linger agonisingly over the final few mouthfuls so that, with careful timing, you will just miss 'last orders'. Alternatively, you can knock it back in double-quick time and, with the others each still having best part of a pint left, announce that you are off home to catch a really interesting documentary about the lifestyle of the spotted flycatcher. By the time you all meet up again, they will have forgotten that you didn't buy a round.

Another method of cadging free drinks is to approach a complete stranger. Every pub has its saddo, the bloke who sits by himself night after night, watching the world go by while drinking halves of lager top. The saddo is easily distinguishable from other members of the human race by his appalling dress sense. This will invariably feature a brightly-coloured tank top – the sort Rod, Jane and Freddie used to wear on *Rainbow* – an anorak with detachable hood and decorated with an assortment of lapel badges, a nylon shirt and stained trousers which come to an abrupt halt two inches above his ankles. He will also boast a hairstyle that looks as if it was cut by the council, possibly a beard to try and make himself look interesting and he will more than likely have a chunky National Rail Timetable spread out on the table in front of him. Closer inspection will almost certainly reveal a personal hygiene problem.

Saddos often live alone with their ageing mum and a cat. They might meet people through work, but are rarely invited out anywhere. Their social life consists of going to annual *Doctor Who* conventions which they attend with a religious fanaticism. More than anything else in the world, they need a friend, someone to talk to. This is where you come in. In return for listening patiently to him droning on about the points problems which have affected the 7.36 from Crewe all week and demanding to know which was your favourite episode of the *Ice Warriors* and why, you are guaranteed free drinks for the entire evening. All you have to do is go over to him and tell him you think you know him from somewhere. You can be as vague as you like – it could be school, the library, Mister Byrite (but probably not the massage parlour in the High Street) – because he will be so delighted that anyone is prepared to admit to knowing him that he will immediately welcome you into his world. And what better way to offer the hand of friendship than by buying you a drink? You can keep this up until he has to go home for his cocoa or you lose the will to live, whichever comes sooner. It goes without saying that you should never go into that pub again or you'll have him hanging on to you for the rest of your life.

Chatting up the Barmaid

Barmaids are notoriously tricky to judge. Since they're paid to be polite and smiley faced, it's often hard to tell whether they're thinking about your wad or theirs. These suggestions should help break the ice, even if it's still in the bucket when it comes down on your head:

- She has had a nasty shock, so you say: 'Do you fancy something stiff... or do you just want a brandy?'

- 'Can I see your baps?'

- 'If I said you had a beautiful body, would you hold it against me?'

The Pool Table

The pool table is an integral part of pub life and has a culture all of its own. It also has a tendency to attract the meanest-looking blokes around who, when wielding pool cues, can become formidable adversaries, particularly if you think the money they've left on the table for the next game has been put there in appreciation of your performance. It is not a tip and therefore it would be decidedly unwise to pocket it. So if you're deliberately going to upset somebody on a pool table, make sure it's one of your mates. There are a variety of ways of doing this:

- Sticking a lump of chewing gum to the chalk so that when he chalks his cue, he ends up with a sticky tip.

- Moving the balls around to your advantage when his back is turned.

- Bribing a girl in a low-cut top to lean over the table directly in his eye-line just as he is about to play a crucial shot

- As a last resort, grabbing his bollocks as he is about to pot the black.

Theme Pubs

Nowadays there are theme pubs for just about every nationality in the world – Australian, Irish, American; there is undoubtedly a Basque Separatist theme pub somewhere, although this would not be quite as exciting as it sounds. The thought of a bunch of hairy Spaniards in Ann Summers gear is definitely one for the connoisseur only. By playing on national traits, it is extremely easy to upset the patrons of these establishments.

In an Irish pub:
- Slag off Dana, *Ballykissangel*, Val Doonican's pullovers or The Corrs.

- Make light of the 1845 potato famine.

- Declare that Guinness tastes like sludge from a blocked radiator.

- End every sentence with 'to be sure'.

- Keep saying 'begorrah' for no apparent reason.

- Announce that you're English.

In a Scottish pub:
- Slag off Billy Connolly, Moira Anderson, Rab C. Nesbitt, Kenneth McKellar, the Krankies and Scottish goalkeepers.

- Shout across the bar that all Scotsmen are tossers... of the caber.

- Compare Iron Bru unfavourably to Tizer.

- Say: 'All Glaswegians are poofters'.

- Declare that porridge is about as appetising as a bowl of watered-down dried dog turd.

- Announce that you're English.

In a Welsh pub:
- Slag off Max Boyce, Harry Secombe, male voice choirs, the Manic Street Preachers and sheep.

- Start a discussion about the demise of the coal industry being a good thing.

- Put a Leonard Cohen track on the jukebox – they'll all top themselves.

- Announce that you're English.

In an Australian pub:
- Slag off *Neighbours*, Michael Hutchence, Kylie and Jason, Rod Hull and Emu, *Sons and Daughters*, the Australian cricket team.

- Enter the bar wearing a convict's uniform.

- Say: 'There are better beaches in Lincolnshire'.

- Announce that you're English.

In a French bar/cafe:
- Slag off French rock music, Sacha Distel, Papa and Nicole, Charles Aznavour, the beret as a fashion accessory.

- Declare that French wine is over-priced piss.

- Enter the bar with a string of onions round your neck.

- Debate that Paris isn't a patch on Basildon.

- Announce that you're English.

In a German bierkeller:

- Slag off Franz Beckenbauer, Kraftwerk, Himmler, Michael Schumacher, German efficiency, *Black Forest Clinic*.

- Say in a loud voice: 'Hurst's shot was definitely over the line'.

- Comment on how suspicious Bavarians look in their lederhosen and silly feathered hats.

- Enter dressed as the Prime Minister and start a chant of 'You can stick your f'ing euro up your arse'.

- Announce (somewhat superfluously) that you're English.

In an American bar:

- Slag off their Presidents, *Friends*, *Seinfeld*, the Beach Boys, ten-gallon hats, Steve Martin, Foreigner, Lassie, fries, their Ryder Cup defeats, Tony Orlando and Dawn.

- Suggest that Mickey Mouse is nothing more than vermin.

- Pretend to be Mexican or Canadian (for some reason the Yanks love the English).

In an English bar:

- Slag off English soccer fans.

- Cheer when England concede a goal.

- Go up to a burly skinhead with tattoos and a Union Jack T-shirt and pretend to be Irish, Scottish, Welsh, Australian, French, German or American.

Saturday night at the Movies

CINEMA, THEATRE OR CONCERT

At the Cinema

The cinema is supposed to be a temple of silence where the audience hang on the every word of the great God before them. In that respect, it's a bit like listening to your father-in-law pontificating about the state of the nation over Sunday lunch... except that Leonardo DiCaprio doesn't have enough protruding nostril hair to stuff a cushion. So the most annoying thing you can do in the cinema is make a noise.

Slurping on the dregs of your non-diet Coke, burping with a ferocity which would drown out the chimes of Big Ben, munching on popcorn, fiddling with sweet wrappers – these can all be amazingly irritating to film-goers, especially when timed to coincide with the action on screen. A hearty crunch on a cheese and onion crisp just as Kate and Leonardo are mid-snog never fails.

If it's a film you've seen before, you can drive everyone mad by revealing the plot in a loud voice. Start off with vague references such as 'this next bit's good' before working up to announcements like 'the killer's hiding in the bedroom'.

In the event of there being a few empty seats scattered around the auditorium, you can make it your goal to sit in every one. When the film gets under way, simply mutter something about the lousy view and go and sit somewhere else. This is particularly rewarding when your move necessitates about 30 people having to stand up and let you past, all the more so if you can manage to tread on a few toes en route. By the time you've reached your destination, rows of people will have lost the plot. Once in your new seat, wait 15 minutes or so until everyone has settled down again and then repeat the procedure to another spot.

Some films are simply unsuited to your needs, especially if you go with somebody more intelligent – i.e. a woman. For example, what is the point in going to see Fellini's *Eight and a half* when you take a size 11? Long, arty films can induce terminal tedium, so relieve the boredom by repeatedly kicking the seat in front. If you are unsure how to do this, just watch any seven-year-old. Or you could take off your shoes, rest your socked foot on the top of the seat in front and waggle your toes in the ear of the courting couple. If you're really feeling adventurous, you may prefer to remove your socks altogether so that all the fluffy bits which collect between your toes fall on to the couple in front's King Cones. But there is a risk of physical injury attached to this manoeuvre, particularly if her boyfriend realizes that the chewy morsel which he's just eaten wasn't chocolate. Yawning loudly and stretching your arms skywards can also be intensely irritating to those around you or you might opt for a nice game of solo I-Spy. No matter how hard the people in neighbouring seats try to concentrate on the film, they will find themselves inexplicably drawn to your game and the chances are that before long someone will call out the answer. An alternative scenario is that somebody will deck you.

A dull experience at the cinema may also be enlivened by making loud, irreverent comments about the actors. Remarks like 'look at the size of those' and 'if you ask me, she needs a good seeing-to' are usually guaranteed to prompt a chorus of disapproval, although you will invariably find an unlikely ally in the mild-mannered social worker in the back row with the cushion on his lap. He would wear a dirty raincoat, but it's so stereotypical.

If all else fails, get on your mobile phone and have a dirty conversation with an ex-girlfriend. Then get her to ring back at regular intervals. With any luck, people will be in such a hurry to escape that they'll leave behind a few bags of sweets.

At the Theatre

Most of the tactics employed to cause disruption at the cinema can also be used in the theatre, but to even greater effect since the performance is live. Heckling celluloid can be a fairly unrewarding pastime, but pricking the pomposity of actors on stage before you is altogether more fulfilling. Obviously any heckling should be done with a certain style – a shout of 'oi, big nose' when a thespian with a particularly prominent proboscis makes his or her entry merely panders to the yob element and is likely to have you ejected before the end of the scene. However a cleverly timed 'he's behind you' during the crucial moment in *Julius Caesar* could reap enormous dividends.

After enjoying popular success in soaps or on children's telly, some performers try to convince the world that they are serious artistes by joining places like the Royal Shakespeare Company and appearing in terribly worthy productions. But it does no harm to remind them of their roots occasionally. So when an actress from Albert Square makes her entrance in Act One, Scene Three of Chekhov's *The Cherry Orchard*, greet her arrival by leading the rest of the audience in a chorus of the theme from *EastEnders*. Similarly, if one of Basil Brush's numerous former sidekicks should turn up heavily disguised in a powerful romantic piece (*Romeo and Juliet* for example), what better way of expressing your appreciation for his seduction technique than a hearty 'Boom Boom!'

Another good ploy for unsettling the performers is to react in all the wrong places. Laugh loudly at a perfectly straight line and you will receive puzzled looks from the rest of the audience and the cast. But a lot of people who go to watch stuff like Ibsen, Chaucer and Shakespeare do so for the snob value. They like to pretend they know exactly what is going on – when in truth, like you, they haven't got the faintest idea. So when you alone laugh at a line, they will be terrified that they have missed the joke, that it has gone over their pseudo-intellectual heads. So before long, they too will all start laughing in the wrong places with the result that an intense drama will end up being treated as a Whitehall farce. You can also throw the actors by suddenly clapping half-way through a scene. Again, the rest of the audience won't know whether to ignore you or join in the spontaneous round of applause. Either way, you will cause uncertainty on the stage as the cast wait patiently for the noise to subside or risk having their next line drowned out.

Most of us are familiar with the songs from musicals like *West Side Story*, *South Pacific* or *Oliver!*. It's not because they're any good, it's just that you hear them in so many different settings that they invade your sub-conscious, in the same way that you instinctively know it is folly to buy washing powder and conditioner separately instead of new Bold. But the one thing you're not supposed to do when sitting through a musical is to join in. So an excellent way of behaving badly at the theatre is to wait for the moody booming solo of "Somewhere", or whatever, and start singing loudly and tunelessly, like the congregation on *Songs of Praise*. Encourage all around you to sing along with you, making the whole experience even more disconcerting for the poor bloke on stage by deliberately getting the words wrong. With the right audience, you can turn the evening into a raucous karaoke night.

Make use of the intervals at the theatre by heading for the bar just before the end of the first act and returning to your seat when the second act is already under way. This will ensure maximum disturbance. An equally irritating diversion can be created by pretending to drop a sweet. Whereas any sane person would simply give it up as a lost cause, you explain that it is the last in your bag of Werthers Originals and you must find it. So you start scrabbling around on the floor, crawling along the row, looking under seats, raising people's legs, clambering over seats, making people stand up, generally making a nuisance of yourself. People will be so keen to find the damn sweet in order that they can get on with enjoying the play that they will join in the hunt. Of course, they will never find the sweet because you didn't drop anything in the first place, but at least you will know who's got the best legs in the audience.

At a Concert

A good rock gig provides its own entertainment, but sometimes you are so keen to get inside a new girlfriend's knickers that you'll allow her to talk you into some really dreary evening in the hope of impressing her. This could take the form of a Polish poetry recital at the library, a lecture on the history of raffia at the church hall, or, worse still, she could have a spare ticket for a folk concert.

On a level of enjoyment from one to ten, a folk concert scores minus six, just above root canal surgery without an anaesthetic. The only way to numb the pain is to get totally rat-arsed (not easy if there's nothing stronger than Appletise at the bar), ignore the concert by bringing your Walkman and listening to something decent, indecently grope your girlfriend or pretend that you are having a really good time. Since the last course of action is the most likely to endear yourself to her, go for it. As everyone is swaying rhythmically, clapping along joyously to "Blowin' In The Wind" or "Puff The Magic Dragon", get up from your seat, go down to the front of the stage and start solo dancing with as much manic energy as you can muster. Arms flailing, head banging, imagine you're dancing to Motorhead's "Ace Of Spades" instead of frolicking in the autumn mist to the gentle tale of a dragon named Puff. At the end of the number, quietly return to your seat and tell your girlfriend: 'That was always one of my favourites.'

Here Comes the Judge

JURY SERVICE

As a decent law-abiding citizen, it is your duty to do jury service and to uphold the fine name of British justice. And it's by no means as dull as it's cracked up to be. On the minus side, you can spend two weeks listening to a string of fairly inconsequential cases which barely warrant a mention in the local papers. Even Bill Clinton would have been hard-pressed to justify military action if Saddam had only been accused of nicking lead off a church roof. On the plus side, it's a short day, there's plenty of time for a couple of pints in the lunch break and you get to see people in a worse position than you. Of course, there's no point in doing jury service if you're going to find defendants innocent and, unless we're talking about a leggy blonde in a short skirt, they all look guilty anyway. If they're scruffy, they look guilty. And if they're in a suit, it's only because their barrister has told them to wear one as a desperate act to impress the court because he knows they're guilty.

Although your aim should be to find all of your defendants guilty, there are four situations where leniency may be exercised:

- If a female defendant strongly indicates that you are on a promise if you get her off (unless she's so ugly that the judge has to point out that she's not actually wearing a stocking mask in court).

- If a male defendant offers you a bribe of a minimum of £500 in return for a not guilty verdict.

- If a male defendant, or his family in the gallery, indicate that your limbs may be at risk if he goes down.

- If all of your fellow jurors are absolutely convinced of the defendant's guilt.

This last point should be remembered at all times since being obtuse is part of the juror's armoury. Among the 12 men and women good and true, there will always be one who fancies himself as a latter-day Perry Mason and who volunteers to be foreman of the jury. If he dogmatically declares that the defendant is guilty, it is your duty to take the opposite course even if the accused was caught emerging from a house in the dead of night dressed in a striped pullover and carrying a bag marked 'SWAG'. This will get right up the foreman's nose and, if you argue your case forcefully enough, you will gradually win over the 'don't cares' (those who got out their knitting during the trial and aren't bothered what happens as long as they get home in time for *Emmerdale*). Once you've won everyone bar the foreman over to your side and wasted a couple of hours, you can avert a miscarriage of justice by suddenly changing your mind and coming to the conclusion that maybe the defendant is guilty after all.

The main man in court is the judge and since on a whim he can charge you with contempt of court, it is not wise to antagonise him too much. So tread carefully if you should decide to:

- Roll back from the pub blind drunk for the afternoon session.

- Make crude hand gestures in court suggesting that you would not be averse to rodgering the female defence counsel.

- Call the judge 'mate'.

- Flirt with the defendant.

- Receive a plain brown package from the defendant's family.

- Fall asleep in court.

- Loudly discuss England's European Championship chances with fellow jurors during the judge's summing-up.

- Shout 'Guilty!' as soon as the defendant appears in the dock.

- Pass a note to a girl juror asking her out for a drink.

- Hire a judge's outfit from a fancy dress shop and wear it in court.

- Wear a walkman in court.

- Have a note passed to the judge which reads, 'Can we knock off early today? I want to finish my Christmas shopping'

- Pass round a can of Special Brew to your fellow jurors.

- Shout 'Hi, Dave' to the defendant (although this is a good way to be excused jury service).

- Arrange to go for a drink with the defendant at the end of the first day of his trial.

- Call the judge a 'boring old fart'.

- Read *The Sun* during the closing speeches.

- Confess that you were the defendant's mystery accomplice.

- Wear a black cap in court and wave a miniature noose at the defendant.

- Start up a chant of 'Going down, going down, going down' when the verdict is announced.

Club Tropicana

IN A NIGHTCLUB

Nightclubs are all about pulling. Sure, you can have a drink or two at the same time, but in places where a pint will cost you the equivalent of the national debt of Finland, you can't afford to overdo it. And it's even worse if you end up buying girlie drinks since girls who've spent the whole evening drinking nothing more potent than Coke suddenly develop a taste for a double Bacardi to go with it. And what do you get for your money? A peck on the cheek and the opportunity to watch her and her mates gyrating around their handbags to the sound of "Agadoo". Well, if you're not going to have any fun, the least you can do is make sure nobody else does either.

19 WAYS OF RUINING YOUR MATE'S CHANCES WITH A GIRL

To Her

1. 'My mate reckons you look just like Hayley off *Coronation Street*.'
2. 'There's a tenner riding on you, darling.'
3. 'You wouldn't think he'd got a seven-year-old daughter, would you?'
4. 'He's just gone to the phone. He has to ring his mum if he's out after ten o'clock.'
5. 'You can't tell it's a glass eye, can you?'
6. 'I don't know how he stands working at that abattoir.'

7. 'My mate reckons you'd be a real babe if you lost a stone or two.'

8. 'You know he won't be able to see you tomorrow because he's only on day release.'

9. 'Noel Edmonds is his hero, you know.'

10. 'So you don't mind the whips and manacles then?'

11. 'If you're lucky, he might give you a lift home in his Lada.'

12. 'He's got all the pan pipe albums.'

13. 'Has he shown you his collection of Jack the Ripper memorabilia?'

14. 'You're so much nicer than all the other old dogs he's copped off with this week.'

15. Stick ice cubes down her bra, saying, 'Him and me, we're great practical jokers.'

16. Stick your tongue in her ear, saying, 'Him and me, we share everything.'

To Him (In Front of Her)

1. 'Did you get off on that charge of indecent exposure?

2. 'Have you had the results yet from the clinic?'

3. 'How's the wife?'

8 INADVISABLE CHAT-UP LINES TO THE GIRL OF YOUR DREAMS

1. 'Hi, you're the girl of my dreams.'

2. 'I'm Steve and I'm a love machine. Wanna feel my engine?'

3. 'Have you got a pound coin for the condom machine?'

4. 'You look like the kind of chick who'd know her way round a pork bayonet.'
5. 'C'mon baby, light my fire.'
6. 'You knock me dead... with your breath.'
7. 'Do you like my medallion?'
8. 'Where you from, you sexy thing, you sexy thing, you? Stoke-on-Trent? Nice.'

If you do strike it lucky in a nightclub, the chances are that it will be with a complete stranger. With only limited conversation possible over the James Brown soundtrack, it's not easy to glean too much information about your prospective date. It's rather like buying a tin of food with no label or an MFI flat-pack with no instructions. You just don't know what you're getting. She could be related to Jeffrey Dahmer, The Boston Strangler or, God forbid, Matthew Kelly. Similarly, she won't know anything about you, thus enabling you to invent a dashing persona, guaranteed to get her knickers round her ankles by the end of the first date. For some reason, women are always impressed by power, sensitivity and danger, so if you can combine all three in your CV, you're on to a winner. Prospective world motorcycling champion who gave it all up to nurse his dying girlfriend is pretty hard to beat. Head lion keeper who collects stamps might also do the trick, but she could be put off by the smell. Still, if the lions can put up with it...

After the ceremonial buying of the drink, the next stage with any potential nightclub conquest is the dance. Apart from those show-offs who look as if they're polishing the dance floor with their bottoms, blokes can be a bit shy about strutting their funky stuff unless they've got six pints inside them. Break wind – yes. Break dance – no. So get yourself well tanked up before the slow smoochie stuff comes on so that your inhibitions go off in the opposite direction to your hands. The most fulfilling form of dancing requires more movement from your groin than your feet while your tongue explores her windpipe and your fingers go for a walk in the black forest. You can't go wrong... unless you do any of the following:

Bad Moves on the Dance Floor

* Groping another girl's botty while dancing with your partner.

* Groping another man's botty while dancing with your partner.

* Dancing like a dervish to all the slow numbers.

* Dropping one and declaring, 'It's better out than in.'

* Belching along to the music.

* Calling her 'Janice' when her name's 'Ingrid'.

* Deliberately bumping into as many other couples as possible.

* Loudly commenting to the nearest bloke, 'I don't think much of yours.'

* Asking the DJ to put on "Grandad" by Clive Dunn.

Having safely negotiated the first hurdle, you can think about arranging that first date. Don't be too quick off the mark – play it as cool as anyone with a permanent hard-on and a leering grin can. That way, she should be gagging for it by the time you get together. But remember, she may get a nasty shock seeing you in daylight for the first time so somewhere with subdued – or no – lighting could be a smart move.

9 INTERESTING VENUES TO SUGGEST FOR YOUR FIRST DATE

1. Your bedroom
2. Her bedroom.
3. Lap dancing at the British Legion.
4. The All-England Darts Finals.
5. A tour of the strip joints of Soho.
6. A slaughterhouse.
7. The Old Bailey.
8. A Rangers vs. Celtic match.
9. A red-light district.

Although nightclubs are generally viewed as the mecca for pulling, other venues can be equally rewarding, such as nurses' balls (if you can wangle an invite), the AGM of the National Association of Strippers (if you get to hear about it) or anywhere that busloads of foreign students with long legs and limited English hang out. Less promising chat-up locations are libraries (unless you're proficient in semaphore), the laboratory where they test the effectiveness of Diocalm, snorkelling clubs, a funeral where she's just buried her husband, a gas-mask wearers' convention and monasteries.

If your reasons for wanting a new girlfriend are purely carnal, nurses are generally reckoned to be the surest bet. After all, with what they have to look at each day, nothing on your body can possibly shock them. Besides, they're used to handling flesh and to patients getting hard-ons when ointment is rubbed anywhere within three feet of their wedding tackle. So all in all, a nurse would be pretty upset if you didn't try it on within five minutes of meeting. The only thing to be on your guard against with nurses is accepting presents of clothing from them. It can be a bit of a dampener to learn that the shirt she gave you had belonged to a bloke whose life support machine was switched off two days before your birthday.

Policewomen are usually up for it too, particularly if you show your caring, sharing side which will come as a refreshing change from some of the neanderthals in CID. Also, policewomen are used to handling helmets. However you should always be mindful that there are certain places you shouldn't take a policewoman on a first date, such as on an armed robbery. Other sections of society present more of a challenge to the would-be suitor. These include:

- Nuns.

- Magistrates.

- The Queen.

- Your mother-in-law.

- Martina Navratilova.

- Anyone with a zimmer frame.

No sooner do you start going out with a girl than, by some remarkable coincidence, she announces that it's her birthday the following week. So what should you buy her?

11 PERFECT GIFTS FOR YOUR GIRLFRIEND

1. An inflatable doll.

2. A phallic-shaped ornament.

3. A six-pack of lager.

4. A year's subscription to *Mayfair*.

5. A framed photo of two horses mating.

6. A framed photo of her parents mating.

7. A framed Xerox of your arse, or any other part of your anatomy.

8. A dozen packets of condoms.

9. A Black and Decker workmate.

10. A set of adjustable spanners.

11. A pregnancy-testing kit.

Sex

Women can be pretty demanding in the trouser department. They treat sex like a six-course meal – they want it to go on all night and still expect you to be able to produce a big tip at the end. Whereas to blokes, sex is like a Chinese takeaway – a quick blow-out and then down the pub to tell your mates about it. If you find yourself embroiled in one of these marathon sessions where the foreplay seems to last longer than a family visit to a deaf aunt, you'll need a few ideas to keep you occupied while your girlfriend is attaining new heights of ecstasy. Always keep the remote control handy so that you can catch *Match of the Day*. As long as you keep the sound down and continue to provide the occasional pelvic thrust every now and then, she'll probably be none the wiser. Obviously you may have to press down a buttock if it's obscuring the last third of the pitch and you may experience a gradual wilting sensation when your team concedes a goal, but otherwise it's a pleasant way to pass the time. Or you could try dropping a gentle hint, along the lines of: 'How much longer are you going to be? I've got a darts match in half an hour.'

21 THINGS TO SAY WHICH MIGHT UPSET YOUR PARTNER AT THE HEIGHT OF SEX

1. 'I must remember to fill in my VAT returns in the morning.'
2. 'You look just like your mother.'
3. 'You're better than your mother.'
4. 'Would you like a crisp?'
5. 'Lorraine used to do that.'
6. 'Have you heard my impersonation of Foghorn Leghorn?'
7. 'Is that it? Can I go now?'
8. 'Did you remember to lock the back door?'
9. 'Sorry about that – it must be those Brussels sprouts.'
10. 'I see the Halifax shares dropped 12 points today.'
11. 'God, I wish you were Ulrika Jonsson.'
12. 'It's my mobile. I must answer it – it'll be Roy saying which pub we're meeting in tomorrow night.'
13. 'Haven't you got funny-shaped ears?'
14. 'Do you mind if I read a book?'
15. 'I fancy pizza for Thursday.'
16. 'I think it's come off.'
17. 'Did you see that picture of Michael Winner in the paper?'
18. 'If I could remember your name, I'd tell you how much

I'm enjoying this.'

19. 'You've got a big bogey hanging from your nose, but don't let it put you off.'

20. 'I think Mr. Floppy's come to visit.'

21. 'Ten green bottles...'

All guys have fetishes, many stimulated by some youthful experience, although getting worked up about rubber after seeing your mum do the washing-up in her Marigolds comes under a different heading altogether. Most fetishes are harmless, but there are exceptions.

Male Fetishes it is Best to Keep Quiet About

- Moira Stuart.

- Parsnips.

- Satanism.

- Pantomime horses.

- Your sister-in-law.

- Lard.

- Inflatable dolls.

- Torvill and Dean.

- Necrophilia.

- Ginger hair.

- Cycle clips.

- Jimmy 'Five Bellies' Gardner.

- Clapham Common.

- Baked bean baths.

- Stuffing oven-ready turkeys.

- Sacrificing virgins.

- John Selwyn Gummer.

Another way to inject a bit of intrigue into your sex life is by getting your partner to dress up. Men tend to go for things which are shiny and plastic. So do women – but it's usually your credit card. Once again, there are some costumes which are best avoided.

Things Not to Ask your Girlfriend to Dress up in for Bed

- An Otis the Aardvark costume.

- A suit of armour.

- A beige anorak.

- A cardigan.

- An Esther Rantzen mask.

- Spiked running shoes.

- A space suit.

- As her mother.

Romance is a vastly overrated commodity, invented by florists to con blokes into parting with large sums of money in return for a couple of wilting carnations. And when you hand them to your girlfriend, she immediately jumps to the conclusion that you've been seeing someone else and are feeling guilty about it. So what's the point? If you had wanted to spend a small fortune just to be miserable, you would have bought a Manchester City season ticket. Anyway, romance is very much a girlie thing. Blokes don't go in for it, or if they do, they give it a different emphasis.

15 EXAMPLES OF WHAT LOVE IS FOR A MAN

1. Love is... her allowing you to come home drunk without delivering a lecture.

2. Love is... her not burning your girlie calendars.

3. Love is... her putting two melons down her top to pander to your Pamela Anderson fixation.

4. Love is... her not calling you an immature little tosser in public, even though it's well deserved.

5. Love is... her allowing you to crack endless insensitive jokes at her expense in front of your mates.

6. Love is... her letting you go to the match while she does the food shopping.

7. Love is... her never criticising your performance in bed.

8. Love is... her allowing you to criticise her performance in bed.

9. Love is... her not complaining about the empty cans of lager strewn across the lounge.

10. Love is... her coming home from work and happily doing all the cooking, ironing and washing because you've had a long, hard day at the pub.

11. Love is... her never mocking the clothes you wear.

12. Love is... her not minding you making helpful suggestions as to how she might improve her dress sense by getting rid of that ghastly green flowery thing and replacing it with a little black rubber number.

13. Love is... her forgiving you for missing Sunday lunch at her mother's because you were engrossed in a game of 'Spin the Bottle' at the pub.

14. Love is... her not minding when you chat up other girls in public.

15. Love is... her rebuffing your mates' drunken advances, saying she wouldn't dream of sleeping with anybody else when she was going with someone as wonderful as you.

You see, this is what love and romance are all about – sharing. But after a while the excitement of a torrid sexual relationship can become too much for you. After all, you can have too much of a good thing – with the possible exception of Special Brew and lamb kebabs. So there may come a time when you want out, but being a caring, sensitive sort of chap, you don't want to hurt her feelings with some cold termination. Subtlety and consideration are the name of the game.

Ways of letting her down gently:

- 'Have you ever thought this flat's a bit cramped for two?'

- 'I've just discovered I've only got three months to live and it simply wouldn't be fair to put you through the pain and suffering.' (This has the added bonus of virtually guaranteeing a farewell shag).

- 'Your suitcase is in the hall.'

When dumping your girlfriend, it is essential to chose your moment carefully. Never make the announcement when she is holding a sharp instrument, driving your car, or has her mouth around your knob. The ideal way to do it is by fax, e-mail or by phone from the airport as you are about to leave the country.

Alternatively, you may think it's kinder if you encourage her to chuck you. Sure, it's a bit of a blow to the male ego and all that, but you can still tell your mates that you kicked her out. The tender approach will ensure that she won't suspect a thing. Here are a few handy phrases:

- 'I'd forgotten quite how pig-ugly you look first thing in the morning.'

- 'So do you still love me, you old slapper?'

- 'You look 18 stone in that nightie.'

- 'I'd rather spend the rest of my life with Barbara Cartland.'

- 'I'm off to boff your friend Lisa.'

She Wears my Ring

AT A WEDDING

Although the course of true love rarely runs much smoother than a rhinoceros's buttocks, the natural progression from that initial nightclub meeting should be towards a wedding day. And, as any man will tell you, the most important part of a wedding is the stag night. Now stag nights aren't much fun if you're the groom – they're just one long night of condemned-man jokes and wondering whether you've made the biggest mistake since King Harold said, 'What arrow?' You are also duty-bound to drink whatever concoction is placed in front of you, even if it looks like something that's come from a weeping boil. If you're lined up for best man duties, however, you can not only get every bit as rat-arsed as the groom (and invariably at his expense), you can also manufacture a level of embarrassment usually reserved for Keith Harris and Orville's singing career.

The first thing to arrange is the entertainment. No stag night is complete without some form of strippagram, but these days there are so many to choose from.

8 STRIP-A-GRAMS TO AVOID AT A STAG NIGHT

1. Pauline Fowler-a-gram (unless you're turned on by cardigans).
2. Librarian-a-gram (unless you're turned on by the sound of silence).
3. School crossing patrol lady-a-gram (unless you're turned on by the uniform and the Tufty Club).

4. Tax inspector-a-gram (unless you're turned on by the thought of coughing up large sums of money).

5. Desert Orchid-a-gram (unless you're turned on by a shovel and bucket).

6. Ena Sharples-a-gram (unless you're turned on by hairnets).

7. Queen Juliana of the Netherlands-a-gram (unless you're turned on by going Dutch).

8. Fatlass-a-gram (unless you're blind).

The most popular choice remains the policewoman – and a wise one it can prove. For most grooms, aware that their mates are planning something, will take one look at a WPC arriving at their stag party and immediately assume that she is a strippagram. So beforehand, nip down to your local police station and try to persuade the sergeant to volunteer the services of one of his best-looking female officers for a few minutes. A small donation to the Police Benevolent Fund might sway things in your favour. When she turns up at the party, the groom, by now well-oiled, will jump to the wrong conclusion and, with any luck, start conducting his own strip search. Before he reaches the point of gasping, 'Hello, hello, hello, what's all this then?' she will produce her genuine ID card. If he still thinks it's a wind-up, the sight of a burly male officer sitting outside in a patrol car may help convince him otherwise.

A stag night has to end with some outrageous act, otherwise the groom might as well have stayed at home playing Scrabble with his maiden aunt. This grand climax usually involves chaining the groom to a lamp-post or some other immovable object.

10 IRRESPONSIBLE PLACES TO CHAIN THE GROOM

1. In a container on a Qantas airline bound for Sydney.

2. Outside a convent.

3. To the barrier on the central reservation of the M1.

4. To the bars of the tiger enclosure at the zoo.

5. To the Rt. Hon. Margaret Beckett, MP.

6. To the foot of the Log Flume ride at Alton Towers.

7. To the top of the Post Office Tower.

8. To a bull.

9. To his future mother-in-law.

10. To Michael Schumacher's Ferrari on the grid of the Belgian Grand Prix.

When the groom is finally freed, he will, of course, swear that he never wants to see you in his life again and that he will kneecap you at the first available opportunity. Think of this as a compliment. You have done your job well.

The wedding ceremony itself is a solemn occasion – sometimes bordering on the tragic – so, as best man, you will need to be a model of restraint, apart from the traditional jest of pretending that you've forgotten the ring. You can milk the moment for all its worth by insisting that you really haven't got it, but it is probably a good idea to stumble miraculously upon the ring before the vicar completely loses his rag and threatens to move on to the next couple. If your role at the ceremony is merely that of a guest in a hired suit, you will naturally find yourself needing to clear your throat at the precise moment when the vicar asks whether anyone knows of any reason as to why this marriage should not take place. Of course, you may be beaten to it by the bride's mother.

In contrast, the groom is very much at the centre stage of proceedings, so if it's you that's getting married, this is your chance to shine. Set down the ground rules for the forthcoming union by turning up late at church, just as the bride's father is standing at the door looking at his watch for the sixth time. The bride will be so relieved that you haven't humiliated her in public, particularly if you come up with some lame excuse about a puncture, that she will readily forgive you. The bride's father may be less forgiving, but console yourself with the fact that it's difficult to book a hitman on a Saturday afternoon. Inside the church, you can push your luck a bit further by deliberating for an eternity before saying, 'I do.' But this rather loses its impact if the bride snaps: 'Well if that's how you feel, I'm off!'

The Reception

Just as the wedding ceremony is made for the groom, so the reception offers the chance for the best man to show his wares. It is customary for the best man to cop off with the best-looking bridesmaid as reward for his endeavours. This alone is the reason for accepting the job in the first place. It is, however, deemed bad form for the best man to try and cop off with the bride. Knobbing her over the trestle table next to the wedding cake will almost certainly produce a few 'tut tuts' from the assembled guests. The only way you can hope to get away with it is if the only other person in the room is a senile aunt who thinks that you're the groom.

Best man duties also require you to make a jolly speech about the happy couple. Whilst your speech will be expected to be mildly irreverent, some things are best left unsaid. These include:

- The fact that the bride is two months' pregnant.

- The fact that the bride is only getting married to get away from her awful parents.

- The fact that the groom spent the night before the wedding with an old girlfriend.

- Details of the groom's criminal record.

- The fact that the bride has always fancied you something rotten – and you've got the scratch marks on your back to prove it.

- The fact that the bride drinks like a fish.

- The fact that the bride's father had to pay the groom to go through with the wedding.

- The fact that the bride is a bit of an old slapper.

But this should still leave you with plenty of ammunition.

- Read your speech from a pair of knickers, saying that they were the only things you could lay your hands on last night, and adding that you'll give them back to the bride afterwards. All except the bride's parents will chuckle at this ribaldry. If it happens to be true, the bride may also look a little flushed.

- When thanking the bridesmaids for their efforts, add that you'd like to thank each one personally in room 235 after your speech.

- Point out that you're sure the groom's medical history will be no bar to the couple's future happiness.

- Enthuse that the groom's liking for unusual sex will stop the relationship from ever going stale.

- Admiring the spread, remark that it must have taken a long time to lay the table – in fact probably twice as long as it takes to lay the bride.

The best man's final duty is to prepare the couple's car prior to departure. This usually involves scrawling messages such as 'Just Married' or 'About to Get Laid' on the windscreen and tying ribbons and tin cans to the rear bumper. If you're feeling particularly cruel, you could go as far as letting down one of the tyres, hiding the car keys down the front of one of the bridesmaid's dresses (and watching the bride fume as her new husband spends two minutes fondling around before deciding that they're definitely not there) or phoning the police to report a drunken driver (giving the registration number of the groom's car). A more imaginative trick is to insert a kipper in the engine, the smell of which will ensure a honeymoon to remember. Of course, if they're honeymooning in Grimsby they probably won't even notice.

6 THINGS NOT TO DO TO THE HAPPY COUPLE'S CAR

1. Saw through the brake cables.

2. Remove the wheels.

3. Remove the doors.

4. Make it into a convertible.

5. Slip a live black mamba under the driver's seat.

6. Tell them, 'Here is your chauffeur – Mr. Knievel.'

Honeymoon

You don't want to get your marriage off on the wrong foot, so there are some items which it is probably best not to take on your honeymoon. Among them are:

- Your ex-girlfriend.

- Your mate.

- Your lawyer.

- Extensive reading matter.

- A family-size jar of haemorrhoid cream.

- A 20,000-piece jigsaw.

- A book entitled *Losing Your Virginity*.

- A book entitled *Impotence Explained*.

- A television listings guide.

- The number of the Gay and Lesbian Switchboard.

- Your mother.

9 NOT TERRIBLY EXCITING PLACES TO GO ON A HONEYMOON

1. Your in-laws' house.

2. Your office.

3. Dungeness Power Station.

4. Spaghetti Junction.

5. A fertility clinic.

6. The nearest Arndale Centre.

7. A tour of a glue factory.

8. The left luggage office at Crewe station.

9. Ante-natal classes.

9 to 5

AT WORK

The Interview

Some things in life are guaranteed to send you rummaging for a fresh pair of underpants – seeing your girlfriend try out your new car, watching the England tail bat, Emily Bishop asking you back to her place. To this list can be added job interviews. For a job you really want, you will do anything to ingratiate yourself with the person on the other side of the desk – you'll laugh at their feeble jokes, agree with everything they say ('you're absolutely right, it is a pathetically sad hairstyle and I do need to get it cut'), even offer to have their babies. But sometimes you go for an interview and pretty soon you realize that Pot Noodle taster would have been preferable to the job you are up for.

10 JOBS TO DIE FOR... NOT!

1. The England manager's PR man.
2. Chief nit inspector at a by-pass protest.
3. William Hague's gag writer.
4. Re-building the Millennium Dome out of phlegm.
5. Head of Tourism for the Dogger Bank.
6. Assistant pooper scooper in Hyde Park.
7. Patrick Moore's tailor.
8. Conducting a penguin census in the Antarctic.

9. Novelty joke salesman in Germany.

10. Lollipop lady on the M1.

In these circumstances, you need to adopt a new interview technique – one which is designed to make sure that you are not offered the job under any circumstances. To achieve this, you need to forget about toadying around like Uriah Heap and be brutally frank with your interviewer.

16 THINGS NOT TO SAY TO A PROSPECTIVE EMPLOYER

1. 'Blimey! Have you just dropped one?'

2. 'Who's that old bag in the photo on your desk?'

3. 'This place is supposed to be a cushy number, right?'

4. 'Do you want to hear about my previous convictions?'

5. 'I never work in the afternoon – I'm too pissed.'

6. 'Where in God's name did you get that tie?'

7. 'Which route do your cashiers take to the bank?'

8. 'Do you mind if I open a window? The stink from your armpits is killing me.'

9. 'Last six jobs I've had, I've walked out with 50 grand in compensation for wrongful dismissal.'

10. 'Want to buy some porno films?'

11. 'I'm only here 'cos there's no racing on the telly today.'

12. 'I bet you've given that secretary one.'

13. 'You want to do something about that acne, mate.'

14. 'I expect at least nine weeks' holiday.'

15. 'Hey, dog breath, what sort of salary will I be on?'

16. 'I quite fancy your job, actually.'

Every office has its range of characters, but there are a group of stereotypes who can be found in almost any working environment.

The Office Lech

The office lech homes in quickly on anything in a skirt and even faster on anyone who's just taken it off. A firm believer in sexual harassment at all times, his fondling, groping, leering, foaming at the mouth, and crude suggestive remarks sometimes unaccountably earn him a bad name. The birds should be flattered by the attention instead of whinging on incessantly about him trying to get his hands inside their knickers. After all, it's not as if it's something they haven't done with their husbands, and he's only after a bit of fun. I. The lech usually wears an abundance of after-shave, nine-carat gold jewellery and trousers which are painfully tight around the crotch. *Ideal job:* The only male employee in a Janet Reger factory. *Unsuitable job:* Selling *Gay News*.

The Siren

The siren is the female equivalent of the lech, a man-hungry predator who makes Jaws look like a three-spined stickleback. In a perfect world, the siren and the lech would get it together and leave the rest of the office in peace, but their sexual appetites are such that, rather like Birds Eye cod fillets, one is never enough. Besides, the lech is no challenge for the siren – she likes to prey on shy, unsuspecting, usually happily married types in much the same way that the lioness ignores the wildebeest with a black belt in kung fu and instead always goes for the really puny one at the back. The siren wears enough cheap perfume to have the same effect on human lungs as mustard gas, along with big ear-rings, a low-cut top, a short skirt and high heels. She may not be perfect, but she's always grateful and if you do cop off with her, at least you know she won't ever hen-peck you about forgetting to put the bin out for the dustmen. *Ideal job:* Madame in a brothel. *Unsuitable job:* Nun.

The Old Boy in the Corner

The old boy in the corner has been there for years. He can remember when the whole of North London was fields and never tires of telling you about it. He joined the company back in the days when a job was a job for life (unless you were caught with your fingers in the petty cash till), but has managed to survive two mergers and three takeovers because everybody at senior management level thought he had retired 15 years ago. He wears a green or beige cardigan, Hush Puppies and invariably smokes a pipe. He also has an unfortunate tendency to leave his flies open after going to the loo, in which case a caring colleague will sidle up to him and whisper: 'The gate is open, but the beast is asleep.' He likes to take a nap around noon and his major decision each day is whether to have two Rich Tea biscuits in the morning or whether to save one for the afternoon. He brings a packed lunch, prepared by his wife, the contents of which have remained unchanged since rationing ended. *Ideal job:* Slumberland tester. *Unsuitable job:* Stunt man.

Ms. Efficiency

Ms. Efficiency can be a frightening figure. Blessed with X-ray vision with which she can spot whether you're sneaking out with an office biro in your pocket at 30 metres, she has dedicated her life to filing and office management. At any given time, she can tell you precisely how many boxes of paper clips should be left in the stationery cupboard. A stickler for punctuation and punctuality, she is perfectly capable of launching a witch hunt to track down a missing reel of sellotape. She wears formidable, dark-rimmed glasses, a minimum of perfume, has her hair in a tight bun and wears both a sensible skirt and sensible shoes. By night, she lets her hair down, puts in her contact lenses, dons tight leather trousers and becomes a raving nympho – at least, that's what the lech reckons from his dreams. *Ideal job:* Traffic warden. *Unsuitable job:* Masseuse.

The Young Virgin

The young virgin is the lost soul of the office. No matter what he tries, he just can't get his end away. He couldn't pull a bird in an aviary. A natural target for the siren, he is too scared to follow up her offers in case his mum finds out. An innocent at large, he can't hold his drink and starts singing "Hava Nagila" after a half of Woodpecker. He wears sweaters with a diamond pattern from BHS and brightly-coloured socks to show that, deep down, there's a raver trying to get out. His mum makes him put on a balaclava in cold weather, which led to him being pinned up against a wall by the local Sweeney on suspicion of being about to turn over the building society in the High Street. He was released when they found that the only offensive thing he was carrying was a Billie CD. *Ideal job:* Anything on the railways. *Unsuitable job:* The CID.

The Yes Man

The yes man is usually a young executive with a whacking great mortgage and a wife with expensive taste who has decided that the quickest way of getting to the top is to crawl to the boss. Nicknamed 'Arse-lickey' by his fellow workers and with a nose that is browner than Red Rum's, the yes man will do anything to get into the boss's good books. This could take the form of personally watering the boss's pot plant, hanging his coat up every morning or giving him hand relief in the gents. Additionally, Mr and Mrs Boss will be invited round for dinner (an invitation which doesn't extend to anyone else in the office), where the yes man will mildly flirt with Mrs Boss, paying her compliments as far-fetched as suggesting that Mama Cass could have carried her weight with style. However he is always careful not to stray across the bounds of decency – actively chatting up your boss's wife with a view to a shag is not a sound career move. After a week or two, he will start imitating the boss, to the point of wearing similar – if not identical – clothes. But this could prove a dangerous move if his boss is a woman. *Ideal job:* The boss's. *Unsuitable job:* Contestant on the yes-no interlude on *Take Your Pick*.

The Spinster

The spinster is the natural soul mate of the old man in the corner. She makes his tea, panders to his every whim and, at Christmas, disappears with him behind the filing cabinets where they exchange stories about the war. They also share an admiration for those witty poems of Pam Ayres. Shy and retiring (but not soon enough), the spinster always wears subdued colours to work (nothing racier than navy blue), but was once spotted in the shopping precinct wearing a bright red anorak – obviously on her way to a hot date. A kindly soul, she will do just about anything you want her to – except die. *Ideal job:* Librarian. *Unsuitable job:* Soft porn actress.

Whilst there may be the odd occasion at work when you're busier than a millipede's chiropodist, careful planning and conservation of energy will create the opportunity for more rewarding pastimes. The great thing about any office is that it's always awash with rumours. Therefore an important part of your job is to embellish these with a few of your own.

11 RUMOURS TO START AROUND THE OFFICE

1. The spinster has a secret love child in Buxton.
2. The lech was seen at *An Audience With Julian Clary.*
3. The old boy in the corner is a war criminal.
4. Ms. Efficiency is a kleptomaniac.
5. The yes man is being investigated by the Vice Squad.
6. The siren watches videos of *Terry and June.*
7. The young virgin has been showing an unhealthy interest in the Hoover attachment.
8. Mr. Tichbourne in accounts is known as Hazel at weekends.
9. Elsie the tea lady has been asked by the Managing Director to prepare a list of people she would make redundant.
10. Mr. Panathinaikos becomes company Chairman over the weekend, so we've all got to wear Greek national costume to work on Monday.
11. Miss Griggs in personnel is growing marijuana in her out tray.

11 RUMOURS TO START ABOUT YOUR BOSS

1. He wears a toupee.
2. He murdered his mother-in-law with an axe.
3. His bottom drawer is filled with empty vodka bottles.
4. He sleeps with his teddy bear called Nigel.
5. He was the only person in the office to get a pay rise last year.
6. He ate the last custard cream.
7. He never misses *Noel's House Party*.
8. He's impotent.
9. He hangs around Scout huts.
10. He's got a collection of Foster and Allen CDs.
11. He started the Great Fire of London.

The New Boy

The arrival of a newcomer at your firm gives you the chance to capitalise on his naïveté and guffaw away in the background while he makes a complete prat of himself. He'll either come to love you for being such a prankster or he'll take a knife to your car tyres. Most offices have initiation pranks, such as leaving a note for him to call Mr. C. Lyon (with the number of London Zoo written underneath – only the really dim will fall for Mr. L.E. Fant) or sellotaping his wrist to his phone while he is making an important call. Otherwise you can simply spread a whole load of false information about your colleagues. After lighting the blue touch paper you retire to a safe distance, although there is still a distinct possibility that you may end up in casualty.

6 LIES TO TELL THE NEW BOY

1. The boss's name is Mr. Fartface.
2. Ms. Efficiency gets annoyed if any member of staff forgets to slap her bottom when arriving for work in the morning.
3. Mr. Rachmaninov in copyright is deaf in his right ear so you have to bellow really loudly in his left.
4. Miss Hall in petty cash thinks she was a rabbit in a former life and likes the newest member of staff to feed her a lettuce leaf at 10.45am sharp.
5. The spinster loves people to talk dirty to her.
6. The boss has got a phobia about the definite article. If you use it in any sentence either when speaking to him or in company letters, he is likely to sack you on the spot.

With careful training, you can encourage the new boy to cover for you during your frequent absences from the office. So while you're over the road at Ladbroke's watching the 3.15 at Kempton Park to see whether your fiver each-way on Glue Factory is going to reap dividends, or swigging a warm glass of Blue Nun with the new looker in bought ledger, he can provide you with an alibi. When sneaking off for any lengthy period of time, it is essential to convey the impression that you're not far away. Leave your jacket over the back of your chair, make your desk look busy. Whatever you do, don't tidy everything away in neat piles as if you've gone home for the day. At the same time, don't leave any incriminating evidence lying around. If a copy of *Fiesta* is left open on your desk, it won't take Poirot to deduce that you're in the nearest toilet cubicle.

Sometimes even the best-laid plans come to grief. Your alarm clock doesn't go off, you're badly hung over, it's raining and anyway your girlfriend's like a polecat on heat, so you don't lurch into the office until half past ten. The boss is on the warpath. There are only so many times your grandmother can die or so many teeth you can have out before you end up looking like a gurner, so you have to come up with some fresh excuse. It is always a good idea to have a few in reserve, in case of emergency.

Inventive Excuses to Tell the Boss for Being Late into Work

- 'My long-lost cousin from Tasmania called round un- expectedly.'

- 'Hurricane Doris made a special detour from Florida to rip off the roof of our house.'

- 'I forgot to put the clocks forward four months ago.'

- 'I had to amputate my girlfriend's left foot with a small hand-saw because the new pair of shoes she bought from Saxone were too tight.'

- 'I saw David Frost on the telly and thought it was Sunday.'

- 'My dog ate my watch and all the clocks in the house. Then I had to take him to the vets to have the one attached to the microwave removed from his stomach.'

- 'I got so engrossed in this Germaine Greer book I completely forgot what time it was.'

- 'I got so engrossed in this Jeffrey Archer book I completely forgot what time it was.'

- 'There was a mix-up with deliveries to the petrol station and I ended up filling up my car with five gallons of hot Bovril.'

- 'I stayed on to watch *The Teletubbies* because I think they can teach us a lot about business practice.'

- 'I missed my train because I got chatting to some Jehovah's Witnesses.'

- 'My girlfriend's parents were wiped out when a mass brawl erupted at a Daniel O'Donnell concert.'

- 'I'm a lazy bastard.'

- 'I was shagging your wife.'

The Leaving Do

The departure of a work colleague is always a sad moment – if only because you're expected to stick a fiver into a collection for some life-form barely one step up from the amoeba. Hypocrisy is very the much the norm on these occasions, just as it is when some third-rate celebrity dies on a Sunday and there is no other news. As euphemisms jostle for position in tribute, some bloke whose career highlight was a walk-on part in an episode of *Never the Twain* becomes 'a sadly underrated comic', a British singer who hasn't had a hit in this country for 30 years is revealed as having been 'huge in Scandinavia', and a deeply unpleasant actor who made everyone's life hell on set becomes 'a perfectionist'. It's the same with leaving dos. Everyone comes out with the usual garbage about how sorry they'll be to see him go when really all they're interested in is getting their hands on his executive swivel chair or his girlie calendar. But if it's somebody you really don't like, you can either spread malicious rumours about why they're going or tell a few home truths on their leaving card... anonymously, of course.

Mean Rumours to Spread at the Leaving Do

For Him

• As well as typewriters, he's been servicing the Chairman's wife.

• He was fiddling his expenses to the tune of £1,000 a year.

• His haemorrhoids are so bad that he's having to get a standing-up job.

• The Managing Director said he had a crush on him so one of them had to go.

For Her

• She's pregnant by Les the maintenance man.

• She was caught giving the boss a blow job.

• She's joining an obscure religious cult who believe that Jesus Christ has been re-incarnated in the form of Jocky Wilson.

Cruel Things to Put on a Leaving Card

For Him

- Good riddance, you two-timing toss-pot.

- At least the office's Tiny Todger of the Year competition will finally have a new winner next year.

- If only I'd known you were gay earlier...

For Her

- I'll never forget last month's party. You were something else. And don't worry – you say you're only a few days overdue.

- Hope your skin complaint clears up.

- Roses are red, violets are blue, I'd have to be pissed to settle for you.

If the leaving party is for a senior company executive, you may get your once-a-year opportunity to create a favourable impression (or otherwise) with the Chairman's wife. Keep plying her with sweet sherry – not only will she think you're incredibly attentive, but with any luck she'll be too sloshed to remember any *faux pas* you may commit.

12 THINGS NOT TO SAY TO THE CHAIRMAN'S WIFE AT A PARTY

1. 'Do you want to share my cream horn?'
2. 'Do you still wear a colostomy bag?'
3. 'You're not quite as ugly as your husband makes out.'
4. 'Have you got any dope on you?'
5. 'You remind me of my granny.'
6. 'Tongue sandwich?'
7. 'I thought you were dead.'
8. 'And you believe him when he says he's working late?'
9. 'Do you mind if I bury my head in your breasts?'
10. 'Senile dementia's a terrible thing.'
11. 'Can I have a pay rise?'
12. 'Would you like another slice of gateau, you deaf old goat? Oh, you wear a hearing aid now.'

School's Out

THE SCHOOL REUNION

School reunions present an ideal opportunity to get your own back on anybody who ever crossed you in the fifth form: the one who stuck chewing-gum to the seat of your new trousers so that you got grounded for a week by your mum; the one who tried to flush you down the bog after games; the one who pissed in your pencil case during double science; and, of course, the one who copped off with Gina McKenzie, the girl of your wet dreams. And that's just the teachers.

These get-togethers are to be cherished if, against all the odds, you have managed to do something with your life. With some schools, this might just mean staying out of jail. From a position of smug superiority, you can face all those who thought you would never amount to much – and who wrote to that effect on your school report – and derive a degree of satisfaction from discovering that the school swot who was top in everything now works on the bins. There will be other certainties: the kid who sold his dinner tickets at an exorbitant profit has become a lawyer; the boy who was always bottom at geography has become a postman; the kid who mumbled incoherently at the back of the class has become a station announcer with Midland Mainline; and the school bully has become a PE teacher.

7 WELL-KNOWN FACTS ABOUT PE TEACHERS

1. They're crap at every known sport.

2. They're pig ignorant.

3. They're hopelessly unfit, mainly because they're smoking fags in the gym cupboard while you're out running round the school playing field in the pouring rain.

4. They have the sexual restraint of the average rabbit.

5. They think crab football should be an Olympic sport.

6. They think climbing wall bars and walking along a ridiculously narrow beam will make you a better person.

7. They're usually poking the PE mistress.

And what about the rest of the teachers? It is somehow rewarding to see that Mr. Judge, the terror of the fourth form, the man who ruled with a rod of iron and the sound of whose approaching footsteps was enough to strike fear into the most wayward delinquent, is now a shrivelled-up, incontinent grey-haired old git who dribbles his food down his tie. And not too surprising to learn that Miss Crippen, the deputy headmistress who hated all boys with a vengeance, is now living in a lesbian commune just outside Godalming.

Then there are the girlies. Have the babes who looked best in school uniforms kept their looks or are there the first signs of a moustache? Did the buck-toothed gargoyle with thick glasses and a brace get a plastic surgery voucher for her 18th and turn into a page three stunner?

Even if your major achievement in life has been four numbers on the Lottery, it is essential to present yourself as a success story at school reunions. In all probability, this will require extensive exaggeration and glamorization of your personal history. If you make the office tea, portray yourself as a captain of industry. If you arrive at the reunion on the number 36 bus, insist that it's only because the Mercedes is in the garage for repairs. If you're caught having a wank in the bog, maintain that it's purely for recreational purposes. Nobody wants to admit to being a failure in front of one's old classmates, so you can bet that everyone else will be manufacturing similar porkies.

Things Not to Admit at a School Reunion

• That you're still a virgin.

• That school days were the best of your life.

• That you're on the dole.

• That you still like Spandau Ballet.

• That you used to have a crush on the caretaker.

• That you still live at home.

• That you've brought your last piece of geography homework with you.

• That this is the first time you've been invited out all year.

• That you've still got your school uniform.

Some school reunions will extend the invitation to your

partner, but this is a temptation to avoid. Even if you've managed to pull Cindy Crawford and are gagging to show her off, keep her under wraps for fear that some envious smart-arse will reveal a potentially damaging piece of information from your schooldays. Some supermodels may well be undeterred by the news that you used to pick your nose in class and flick bogeys at the blackboard, but they will surely be put off to hear that you were doing it at 18. So rather than risk your relationship, settle for bringing a photograph of your beloved. Obviously if it is some item of hot totty, make sure the photo shows the pair of you – preferably in a state of undress – otherwise nobody in their right mind will believe you. If you are still a solo artist, or your girlfriend is less than easy on the eye, cut out a photo of some luscious bird from a magazine and pass her off as your partner. Obviously choose with discretion. A photo of Anthea Turner might be a bit of a give-away, as might one of a naked woman with a black strip over her eyes, so choose some obscure telly presenter that nobody's ever seen instead – somebody who introduces the sport on Channel 5 at half past two in the morning. That way, you'll only be uncovered if one of the kids in your class went on to be a shift-worker, a night-watchman or a burglar.

With no risk of you yourself being subjected to acute embarrassment, the way is now clear for you to inflict damage on others, especially those who were foolish enough to bring their partners. And the booze is usually free, so get stuck in and make merry.

15 WAYS OF BEHAVING BADLY AT A SCHOOL REUNION

1. Remind people of their old school nicknames, particularly if they're offensive like 'Dumbo', 'Fatty', 'Smelly', 'Tiny', 'Licey', 'Sexually Transmitted Diseasesy'.

2. In front of his respective spouse, remind Nigel Pratt how you once caught him with his head up Jennifer Golightly's dress during French oral.

3. Knee a geriatric teacher in the groin with the message, 'That's for giving me a detention in the third year.'

4. Turn up with a rubber cervical device on your head and announce, 'It's my school cap.'

5. In front of a girl's partner, declare loudly: 'And to think she used to be known as the school bike!'

6. Go up to a girl and say, 'I'm sure I've seen your picture in a magazine. Wasn't it *Readers' Wives*, January 1996?'

7. Make a drunken pass at the Headmaster's wife.

8. Reveal that it was Daniel Moffat who put the gerbil down Cynthia Snape's dress in double maths.

9. Say to a particularly prim girl with her husband standing next to her: 'Come on, darlin', show us your jugs – for old time's sake.'

10. Boast about your GCSE history results.

11. Go up to a female teacher and drool: 'If there's one person I'd have liked to have got the cane from, it's you.'

12. Insist on organising a game of Kiss, Piggy, Kiss.

13. Make suggestive remarks with two pickled onions and a gherkin.

14. Try and play tonsil hockey with every girl present.

15. Lurching aimlessly from side to side, launch into a lager-fuelled soliloquy of passion: 'Ah, Gina, my favourite girl. I've never forgotten you, you know. I remember when you used to sit in front of me during French and when you bent over to pick up your satchel, I could see your knickers. Little pink ones they were, with a butterfly on. Ah, it was heaven. You don't know how much I wanted to get inside them. And you had the best breasts in the class. Lovely and firm and round they were. I wanted to hibernate in your bra for the winter, Gina, and lose myself in your ample bosom. Oh. So which one's Gina then?'

Dedicated Follower of Fashion

GOING SHOPPING

Shopping for clothes from time to time is one of life's unavoidable necessities – like kissing aunts who have got three days' growth of stubble, or being polite to men with Rottweilers. There does come a time, however, when you have to admit that that your T-shirt has finally gone out of fashion, not to mention fallen apart. Most men hate shopping for clothes since it wastes valuable drinking time and, anyway, trying things on is such a chore – unless it is a condom. So you tend to cut corners and guess that clothes will fit you, only to discover when you get home that the jeans you've bought will show half your arse, leaving you with the condition known as 'builder's bottom'. If you can't find anything to fit, the least you can do is make sure that nobody else can either. So when you go back to the shop, browse awhile, taking the opportunity to swap all the clothes around. Take two pairs of jeans of different sizes and then replace them on each other's hangers. Carry on like this until the assistant starts getting suspicious, by which time all the 32-inch waist hangers will hold every size but 32-inch waist jeans. It might seem petty and mean-spirited, but isn't that what life's all about?

Shop assistants are paid to be your humble servants and, as such, should be treated like dogs. Since they leap on you the moment you enter their shop and give the impression that they would kill their granny for the sake of a sale, you should give them the chance to expend a little of their seemingly boundless energy. If you've got a bit of time to kill before the pubs open, take a couple of shirts into the changing cubicle, draw the curtain and pretend that you are trying them on with a view to purchase. After a few minutes, the helpful assistant will inquire anxiously, 'Is everything all right, sir?' Quite what they think can happen to you in a 3ft square area where the only implement is a wall hook remains a mystery. Perhaps you have inadvertently strangled yourself with the sleeves of the shirt, maybe you have been abducted by aliens or have dissolved into a pool of green liquid. In reply to the question, humour him by saying that you really like the style of the shirts but you're not sure about the colour and ask him whether he could bring something else. Hand him back the originals, crumpling them a little first to make it look as if you have tried them on, and wait for the next two. And so it goes on. Get him to bring you every shirt colour in stock and when he's exhausted his supply, try a different style. But remember to maintain his enthusiasm by constantly hinting that you are on the verge of buying one or both. 30 shirts later, when the pubs are about to open, emerge from the cubicle and inform the hapless assistant that maybe you'll come back another day.

By contrast, girls think clothes shopping is a pleasure comparable to a multiple orgasm. And if you've got a new girlfriend, you're expected to tag along too as a gesture of commitment. Since these shopping expeditions usually take place on a Saturday afternoon when you'd normally be at the match, you are making just about the ultimate sacrifice. So you trail around shop after shop, hoping to catch a glimpse of *Grandstand* as you are hustled past Currys. With careful planning, you can make sure that around full-time you're in a big department store with an electrical section. While she's trying on her 58th pair of shoes, you can sneak off to watch the footie results in company with dozens of other men in a new relationship. It's uncanny the number of blokes who suddenly become interested in buying a telly at a quarter to five on a Saturday afternoon...

But apart from that, it's one long trail of clothes shops, punctuated by the occasional hint that your aching feet need refreshing with a pint. This suggestion will more than likely be met with a frosty stare or a packet of corn plasters. And it's worth bearing in mind that comments such as 'a size 8, you must be joking' will merely serve to prolong the agony, but every cloud has a silver lining and it's worth considering the benefits which places like Top Shop have to offer. Where else can you watch the tastiest totty in town take all their clothes off without being arrested? True, there's a curtain in the way, but that doesn't stop you fantasizing. Anyway, it never fits properly, so by craning your neck, you can often gain a quick glimpse of thigh or buttock and, if you edge close enough, you can overhear any conversations such as 'it feels so smooth against my breasts' and 'these really cling to my pert little bottom'. This should be ample compensation for not knowing how United are getting on. However, remember to wipe away any saliva before your girlfriend steps out of the cubicle next door.

If you're lucky enough to have a girlfriend who's got a thing about doing it in public places (such as the Chelsea penalty area during a home match or in the window of C&A), she may invite you into the changing cubicle for a quickie. The notices outside only go on about 'no more than two items' and 'no food and drink' – there's nothing about 'no rodgering'. Of course, while the pair of you are at it like knives (taking care to stifle any moans and groans and not to get bodily fluids over the dress she's supposed to be trying on, unless she is planning to bump into an American President), the assistant will be hovering in the vicinity and will be expecting your girlfriend to answer her questions.

> 'Does it fit?'
> 'Y-e-e-s.'
> 'Would you like a larger one?'
> 'Oh, yes please.'
> 'It will shrink in the wash.'
> 'I know.'

If, on the other hand, your girlfriend is not one of life's natural exhibitionists, you can always wile away the time she is in the cubicle by chatting up the sales assistant. If your girlfriend emerges unexpectedly and wants to know what you're up to, tell her you were trying to negotiate a reduction.

Lingerie Shopping

When it comes to presents, there is supposed to be more pleasure in giving than receiving. Fair enough, but you can heighten the pleasure by buying your girlfriend something that you will make you feel extra horny – such as sexy lingerie. Places like Knickerbox are one type of shop where men are quite happy to browse for ages, tenderly fondling the merchandise. Of course, the sales assistants are wise to this and so if you leave your thumbprints on too many garments, they are likely to have you escorted from the premises by some burly security guard. The key to success is to come across as a shy, embarrassed, decent, stable individual who has never shopped for ladies' underwear before, rather than as a Grade One pervert. Thus first impressions are all important. There are certain things you shouldn't wear when going into a lingerie shop.

- A dirty raincoat.

- A T-shirt with an erect penis on it.

- A T-shirt with 'I'm a pervert' on it.

- A balaclava (this applies to most shops).

- A smile.

By putting on the helpless, lost-little-boy act, you may even manage to persuade the assistant to try on some of the items for you – just so you can see what a black lacy G-string or a leather thong look like on a real woman. It's a bit of a long shot, but you've got nothing to lose.

Supermarket Sweep

Despite claims that supermarkets are the new pick-up joints, most establishments appear distinctly unpromising outlets for all that excess testosterone. You may be lucky enough to catch sight of an item of 24-carat babe bending over the freezers in search of that elusive packet of broccoli, but more than likely it will be some old biddy with wrinkled stockings and one of those lethal pull-along shopping baskets on wheels. Basically, if you're looking for a chick with her own teeth, forget supermarkets – particularly the cheapo ones. So with nothing much worth looking at, you have to take your pleasures another way.

8 WAYS TO AMUSE YOURSELF IN A SUPERMARKET

1. Go round swapping the price stickers on tins and packets. This will create such mayhem when you reach the check-out that you might save yourself a few quid.

2. Take nine items through the 'eight-items-or-less' till.

3. Pile far more items into your trolley than you have any intention of paying for. When the bill comes to £68.25, sheepishly reveal that you've only got a fiver. Simply say, 'I won't bother' and leave.

4. Push the supermarket trolley around at breakneck speed, as if you were Damon Hill. Cut other shoppers up on the corners, overtake on the inside where there's barely room to squeeze through and weave your way up and down the aisles. Time yourself, thereby setting a target to beat for next time.

5. If you and a mate have both got shopping trolleys, have a game of dodgems, deliberately aiming yours at his.

6. Another game for two or more players is to steer your trolley into as many shoppers as you can: five points for a back of the leg; ten points if you emerge from the collision with a piece of your victim's skin attached to the front grill of the trolley; 15 points for drawing blood; 20 points for a blow above the waist and a six months' suspended sentence if your victim has to be rushed to hospital.

7. Take a bite out of apples, strawberries etc as you go round, just to determine whether or not they are ripe.

8. Confronted with a display tower of non-breakable items (such as toilet rolls), remove one from the bottom so that the whole lot comes crashing down. As trolleys are forced to brake sharply and shoppers dive for cover, quickly distance yourself from the scene.

Doctor Doctor

AT THE DOCTOR

Doctor's waiting rooms. They're awful places, full of sick people or screaming kids who'd rather be at home watching *Postman Pat*. And, even if your doctor operates an appointment system, you always have to wait an eternity. Your only hope is that the old dear in front of you dies so that you can take her turn. If you're not pissed off by the time you arrive, you soon will be because the walls are covered with posters vividly describing the symptoms of every potentially fatal disease in the world. You come in with a sore throat and leave convinced you've got beriberi. Why not cheer the place up with a few girlie calendars instead?

And the only person who can get a decent pint in a doctor's waiting room is a vampire. You'd think they could at least put on some supermarket own-brand lager– it's not as if anyone's going to get rat-arsed on that. But what have they got as entertainment? A few Lego bricks for you to trip over and break some bones, a couple of tropical fish which are about as interesting as most fish are without a portion of chips, some back copies of *Woman's Realm* with the problem page missing and an edition of *Homes and Gardens* which is so old that the interior design feature is on the Colosseum. Not a *Mayfair* or *Penthouse* in sight.

Yet, strange as it may seem, there are more depressing places than a doctor's waiting room, such as:

- A manic depressives' Christmas Party.

- A Doncaster Rovers' board meeting.

- A country and western concert.

- A Betamax users' convention.

- A temperance society meeting.

- A Baccara recording session.

- A Sinclair C5 owners' club get-together.

- A script meeting for *The Shane Richie Experience*.

Sadly, a   doctor's waiting room doesn't offer much potential for pulling either. Even if there is a ripe looking girlie who stirs things in the one-eyed trouser-snake department, it is advisable to approach with caution since you don't know what's wrong with her. Looking at things on a purely practical basis, there's not much point in asking her out for a date Monday week if she's expected to croak it this Friday. Worse still, she may be seeking treatment for some sexually transmitted disease, and it might be the one you haven't had yet, so it's best to steer clear. Besides, what would your opening gambit be? 'What's wrong with you then?' It could open the floodgates to half an hour of her full medical history, complete with diagrams. No thanks.

There's always the receptionist, but she's normally matronly with an exterior as forbidding as Fort Knox. Still, if you relish a challenge...

Basically, you've got 40 minutes to kill and bugger all to do. There must be something.

13 THINGS TO DO IN A DOCTOR'S WAITING ROOM

1. Tell everyone you've got some dreadfully contagious tropical disease and watch them all flee the waiting room, leaving you to go in next.

2. Ask all the patients what they've got wrong with them and tell them how long you reckon they've got left to live. Be prepared for adverse reactions to any diagnosis of 'less than an hour'.

3. Fake a sudden wheezing and coughing fit and start writhing around on the floor so the receptionist hurries you in next.

4. Pull faces at the tropical fish.

5. Pull faces at the receptionist.

6. Feed bits of your scab to the tropical fish.

7. Build a set of male genital organs out of Lego and then show your handiwork to all the old dears.

8. Do the crossword in the September 1993 edition of *Country Life*, filling in 'sheep shagging' as the answer to each clue.

9. Before leaving home, wrap a bandage around your hand and smear it with over-ripe banana and a hint of tomato ketchup so that it looks as if the non-existent wound beneath the bandage is seeping. Show it to everyone in the waiting room, especially those who look to be of a nervous disposition.

10. Try the old glass eye trick. Put a marble in the same pocket as your handkerchief and lift them out together, concealing the marble in the handkerchief. Then when you're sure that at least one person in the waiting room is watching you, pretend to remove your eye from its socket and to put it on the handkerchief. Keep that eye firmly shut, produce the marble and polish it furiously with the handkerchief. As people are about to throw up, flourish the marble and appear to push it back into the socket. When you open your eye again, keep the marble hidden in your hand. This trick may be difficult to pull off in front of an alert audience, but the crowd you get in a doctor's waiting room will be ideal.

11. Tear out the photo of Camilla Parker-Bowles from *Horse and Hound* and, using spit as an adhesive, stick it on to Arkle's body. See if anyone notices the difference.

12. Announce that there's a nasty dose of Asian flu doing the rounds. The thought of any foreign viruses always puts the wind up the old folks.

13. Fart away relentlessly as if re-creating the baked beans scene from *Blazing Saddles* and apologise profusely for the appalling smell. With any luck, the other patients will insist that you go in before them.

It's Getting Better

IN HOSPITAL

The prospect of spending several days in hospital is distinctly unappealing. For a start, unless you happen to be in a particularly enlightened branch of the NHS, the chances are that your ward won't have a bar, and it's sod's law that instead of getting a nurse with a warm smile and a welcoming bosom, you'll get one with hairy legs and a moustache. Male nurses! They're no more welcome in hospitals than a recurrence of the Black Death, but short of forming an escape committee, there is no way out, so you'll just have to make the best of a bad job.

The first thing to do is to make sure you are always attended to by the prettiest nurse on the ward. When the male nurse asks you whether everything is OK, just nod, because the last thing you want is his hands ferreting about beneath the sheets, but when a female nurse who is positively bursting out of her uniform passes by, complain about a pain in the groin. Even though she may think the pain is more in the anal region, she will be obliged to check. The sensation of those gentle hands refreshing the parts that others cannot reach will make for sheer ecstasy, although you should bear in mind the fact that the moment may be tarnished somewhat if you accidentally "unpop your cork".

Assuming that you manage to contain yourself, you'll be wanting to chat her up. For a half-decent-looking nurse this is an occupational hazard. It could take more than a grape to win her affections. The trouble is, she'll have heard every pathetic attempt at witty repartee a million times before, so you might as well forget the Woody Allen stuff and just be direct. 'Fancy a shag?' will at least let you know where you stand and leaves little room for misinterpretation.

If you draw a blank on the nursie front, you're not left with much to make your stay in hospital bearable, but there are several ways of easing the pain. For example:

- Get your mates to smuggle in cans of lager. (This is not advisable if alcohol poisoning is the reason for your hospitalization).

- Get your mates to smuggle in girlie magazines. (This is not advisable if you are in with high blood pressure or for treatment to combat premature ejaculation).

- When the patients gather in the television lounge to watch *Last of the Summer Wine*, switch over and make them sit through a documentary about fatal medical blunders.

- Volunteer to adjust the traction position of the man in the next bed.

- Turn your radio on full volume in the middle of the night, explaining that you can't sleep.

- Help yourself to the other patients' chocolate when they go to the loo.

- Complain about the hospital food and ask whether there's any chance of a bit of smoked salmon.

You might also find yourself in hospital as a visitor to a sick friend or relative. Given that he or she will be bored stiff by hospital life (there is however a fine distinction in hospital between being bored stiff and being a bored stiff), liven things up with your visit. Bring a present of rubber grapes or a bunch of flowers which bursts open to say 'Boo!', although remember the latter joke may lose its edge if the patient goes into cardiac arrest. Alternatively, put the bedside lamp shade on your head and pretend that you are Frankenstein's monster coming to life. Be prepared to curtail your performance if you see too many patients cowering under the sheets. In view of the patients' general fragile physical and mental state, it is best to be diplomatic during hospital visits and not say anything likely to upset the patient. But when have you ever been diplomatic?

16 COMMENTS WHICH MIGHT UPSET A SICK RELATIVE

1. 'I heard the sister say that three people died on this ward alone last night. They reckon you're lucky to get out of here alive.'
2. 'I like your watch. Can I have it if you don't pull through?'
3. 'You look like death warmed up.'
4. 'The staff here don't look as if they know what they're doing. It wouldn't surprise me if they're getting the patients' prescriptions mixed up.'
5. 'Mrs Wicks at number 41 had the same symptoms as you. They buried her yesterday.'
6. 'Sorry to hear about your dog. Oh... you didn't know?'
7. 'You'd be better off dead than stuck in here.'

8. 'You want to be careful with that hospital food. You never know what they're giving you. Could be dog food for all you know.'

9. 'Your house burned down last night.'

10. 'The smart money says you've got two weeks.'

11. 'You can almost smell death in the air.'

12. 'Oh by the way, if you're wondering why your wife hasn't been in to visit, it's because she's left you.'

13. 'I overheard the nurses saying, "He'll never walk again." Of course, they might not have meant you.'

14. 'Have you made a will?'

15. 'I didn't bring you any flowers because I wasn't sure whether you'd still be alive and they'd only go to waste.'

16. 'And what's this tube attached to? Oops, sorry.'

Or you could be visiting your wife after she's just given birth. Again, she will be in a highly emotional state of mind and might not appreciate any of the following remarks:

• 'God, you look fat.'

• 'Are you sure he's mine?'

• 'I can't wait to have you home – there's a stack of washing to do.'

• 'He looks uncannily like the milkman.'

• 'I hope you get your figure back soon or I'll be looking elsewhere.'

- 'I'm glad you've had a nice rest because I've been really busy.'

- 'We had an all-night party last night. The place is in a right state.'

- 'You know your favourite ornament, the one your mum bought you? I'm sure it can be mended.'

- 'Look, he's got your nose. Still, plastic surgery's a wonderful thing.'

- 'I've been made redundant – what a time to have another mouth to feed!'

- 'He's an ugly little bleeder. Can't we swap him for a baby that's easier on the eye?'

Going Underground

ON PUBLIC AND PRIVATE TRANSPORT

6 WAYS TO IRRITATE YOUR FELLOW UNDERGROUND PASSENGERS

1. Eat loads of garlic the night before. Why not? Everyone else seems to.
2. Let a long, smelly one go just as the doors close, thereby sealing in all the aroma and flavour.
3. Insist on entering into meaningful conversations with your fellow travellers, all of whom wish to retain their anonymity. Possible subjects include: the mating habits of the three-toed sloth; the joy of lager; and pissing into the wind.
4. Gob all over the floor of the carriage.
5. Pretend you are a colour-blind foreign tourist and ask for directions to Alperton or some destination which requires a couple of changes. As your reluctant guide tries to explain that you change from the black line to the red line to the blue line, your colour blindness comes into play, creating a wealth of confusion. Choose your victim carefully, however, or you may annoy him or her so much that you find yourself wearing the sand bucket on your head.
6. Keep saying 'Mind the gap' whenever the train stops at a station.

9 WAYS TO BE A NUISANCE ON MAINLINE TRAINS

1. Read your newspaper out loud.
2. Read the newspaper of the person sitting next to you out loud.
3. Ask the person opposite you whether he'd mind holding his newspaper a little higher so that you can read the racing results.
4. Ask the person opposite if you can borrow a few pages from his newspaper while he is still reading it.
5. Insist on helping the person next to you with his crossword.
6. Although you've got your Walkman on, sing along audibly to the music.
7. Breathe heavily on the window and make rude drawings with your fingers.
8. Return from the buffet with half a dozen packets of crisps and crunch them loudly in the face of the businessman trying to prepare an important speech on his portable computer.
9. Accidentally-on-purpose spill the contents of your bag of mixed nuts and raisins on to the lap of the blonde sitting next to you and attempt to remove them individually by hand. They'll taste better, too.

6 BLATANT LIES TO TELL ON A TRAIN

1. 'The food from the buffet is such good value.'

2. To a female ticket collector: 'You've got a nice arse.'

3. To a male ticket collector: 'Your personal hygiene standards are exceedingly high.'

4. 'This service is always punctual.'

5. 'Travelling into London by train from Southend is so relaxing.'

6. 'No, you never hear anybody with a mobile phone.'

Air Travel

The great thing about flying is that getting pissed is almost compulsory. Nobody sober would ever even contemplate going up in a plane, so air companies virtually recommend that you have a drink beforehand to steady your nerves, and if you're a particularly nervous sort, you may need five or six. Then on most flights, once you get on board, they bring round the free booze trolley. What more could you ask from in-flight service? Of course, the air stewardesses, flight attendants, shag-happy crew or whatever it is they call them these days won't serve you with alcohol if they think you've already had enough to drink, so it is important to present a sober front. This may prove tricky, but it can be done. To convince the crew that you are the model of sobriety, don't:

- Throw up in the aisle.

- Ask the stewardess to marry you.

- Tell the woman opposite she could be a real looker if she

put the sick bag over her head.

- Inflate the life-jacket and blow the whistle for a laugh.

- Scream 'we're going to crash, we're going to crash', before the plane has even begun to taxi.

- Start dancing wildly to the music on the headphones.

- Ask the stewardess whether she's a member of the mile-high club.

- Tell the pilot he's your best friend.

- Insist that the in-flight magazine is a really good read.

In addition to overloading your bladder, planes are also excellent places for pulling. Unfortunately when you book your seat, you only get the choice of 'window' or 'aisle', and not 'stuffy businessman' or 'micro-skirted babette'. However, if you should be lucky enough to find yourself seated next to a potential goer, don't waste the opportunity. For once in your life, you've got a captive audience. Even if she hasn't got her seatbelt on all the time, she can't escape very far – you really must be incurably dull if she announces she's going for a walk up and down the aisle. Furthermore, you can prey on her girlie worries of flying. If you can instil the fear of God into her, you'll end up with her head on your shoulder for the next three-and-a-quarter hours, her luscious lips begging you to stroke her brow and soothe her troubled breasts. At least, that's the theory.

12 THINGS TO SAY ON A PLANE TO PUT THE WIND UP A GIRLIE

1. 'Did you read about that terrible plane crash in Chile?'
2. 'Were those flames I saw coming from the engine?'
3. 'That stewardess looks as if she's shaking. I wonder if she knows something.'
4. 'That's the exciting thing about flying – disaster can strike at any second.'
5. 'Look around you at all these people. If this plane were to plummet out of the sky, none of us would stand a chance. We'd never see our loved ones again. It's something to think about, that.'
6. 'I saw the pilot knocking back the brandies before we took off.'
7. 'The engine seems to have cut out.'
8. 'I wonder what happens when an air traffic controller's in a bad mood, when he's had a row with his missus and just doesn't give a damn.'
9. 'If we were all to die in the next five minutes, the good thing is it would be sudden. It must be better than being maimed for life.'
10. 'Was that the pilot I saw appear ashen-faced at the cockpit door?'
11. 'The last time I flew on this route, we were lucky to get out alive.'
12. 'It's marvellous isn't it, the technological expertise that defies all the odds and somehow keeps this thing from falling to the ground, bursting into flames and shattering into a thousand pieces?'

If the Kids are United

WORLD OF SPORT

Football

In spite of all the girlies who suddenly profess to be interested in the game because they fancy Jamie Redknapp or David Beckham, football has always been a man thing. Anyway, where were all those groupies when Peter Beardsley was in his prime? The whole point of going to a football match is to be with your mates, get behind your team and gloat at the misfortune of the opposing supporters – not to the point of inciting violence, of course, but a spot of gentle taunting never did anybody any harm. Any taunts should be loaded with satire and irony and should cut rival fans to the quick as if delivered by the Dorothy Parker of the Stretford End, but subjects such as religion or air crashes should definitely be avoided. Most clubs have their own separate identity.

Arsenal   Traditionally as boring as the omnibus edition of *The Money Programme*, while one or two of the players are alleged to have handled more dodgy substances than HM's Customs. Recently became a laughing stock on account of their non-flying Dutchman.

Aston Villa   Fans talk with Brummie accents. Nuff said.

Barnet   Can't even manage a flat pitch.

Barnsley

Hordes of celebrity fans: Michael Parkinson, Dickie Bird, Geoffrey Boycott, probably Arthur Scargill and flat-capped miners who race whippets and keep pigeons in t'loft. After spending nearly 100 years trying to get into the top division, they finally made it, only to go straight back down again. Shame.

Birmingham City

Only redeeming feature is a leggy Managing Director. Doubtful whether she'll do the business just to put one more on the gate though.

Blackburn Rovers

Bought the League title.

Blackpool

Stanley Matthews could still get a game for them.

Bournemouth

No fans under 70. The invalid enclosure takes up three-quarters of the ground.

Brighton

Gordon Smith. Say no more.

Bristol City

Once managed by Alan Dicks, but yokel fans missed out on the chance to sing, 'Dicks Out!'

Cardiff City

Welsh.

Carlisle United   Must be sheep-shaggers from up there.

Charlton   Nice boys.

Chelsea   David Mellor claims to be their number one supporter. Probably also the best-looking. Before Mellor, the best-known chopper in a Chelsea strip was Ron Harris who earned the sobriquet on account of the strength of his tackle.

Crewe   Ground so small it's impossible to have a meaningful sexual encounter on the terraces without getting trodden on.

Crystal Palace   Girlie team.

Derby County   Like Bristol City, their fans missed the chance to berate manager Arthur Cox with chants of 'Cox Out!'

Everton   Scousers.

Grimsby Town   That lovely familiar fishy smell.

Huddersfield Town   Never mind the football team, the club's Rugby League side used to rejoice in the nickname of the Fartowners. Enough said.

Leeds United Play in all white so are the first team to show signs of nerves.

Liverpool *see Everton.*

Luton Town Play in orange. When they defend a corner, they look like a bag of satsumas.

Manchester City The Samaritans of soccer – a comfort to everyone. Your grandad's died, you've lost your job, your girlfriend's run off with your best mate, your lottery numbers came up the week you forgot to do it, you've run out of lager, but things could be worse, you could be a Manchester City supporter.

Manchester United Girlies have loved United ever since they pondered on how 'Nobby' Stiles acquired his nickname.

Middlesbrough Spent millions on Brazilians who couldn't settle on beautiful Teesside. Wonder why that was?

Millwall Once had a player called Jack Cock. He always rose to the occasion.

Newcastle United Never quite made it, despite jolly geordie fans.

Northampton Town Cobblers.

Nottingham Forest Used to have some Scandinavian chappie called Einar Aas. He insisted it was pronounced Orse, as in Orsenal no doubt.

Portsmouth Dodgy place to stand on the terraces with all those sailors behind you.

Queens Park Rangers Specialized in players with silly names such as Mike Bottoms and Arthur Longbottom, not to mention Stan Bowels (Bowles).

Sheffield Wednesday Their star defender used to be Peter Shirtliff. Wonder what his fan club called themselves?

Shrewsbury Town How can you take seriously a team that plays at Gay Meadow?

Swansea City *See Cardiff.*

Tottenham Hotspur Flash gits.

Watford The pubs serve piss poor beer.

York City Worth a mention for once having a player called Arthur Bottom.

The other main pleasure to be derived from a football match is abusing the referee, in the same way that you and your mates crowd round the telly with a six-pack and pull the Miss World contestants apart. But refs get subjected to so much vitriol that it would take more than a cry of 'scraggy legs' or 'fat arse' to send them running to the nearest therapist. Here are some other insults which are unlikely to cut much ice with the man in black:

- 'Oi, ref, your hair's going grey.'

- 'Oi, ref, the crease in your shorts isn't straight.'

- 'Oi, ref, you've got a slightly effeminate run.'

- 'Oi, ref, I bet your wife's holding a cheese and wine party with a few friends at the moment.'

Nothing is more annoying than if your mate has managed to get to the match but you've been otherwise detained – on that Saturday afternoon shopping expedition, perhaps. The solution is simple. Phone the ground and have a half-time announcement put out for him over the tannoy, asking him to return home immediately.

Women will do anything to stop their men going to the match. Some will even get pregnant just so that they can make you miss a home game by attending the birth. Don't fall for it. Here are some very good reasons why it's more important to go to the match than attend the birth of your first-born:

- You can always get her pregnant again – but next time plan it so that she drops during the cricket season. (*note:* beware of World Cup and European Championship years).

- It's an important end-of-season battle with the difference between finishing 12th and 13th.

- You'd only be in the way.

- You'd only be pacing up and down the ward fretting about the result.

- You've been squeamish about births since watching *Alien*.

- You'll be at the hospital by six o'clock anyway – unless it's a good win and you stop for a few pints on the way.

- Your team are unbeaten in three matches.

Playing football offers even greater possibilities for behaving badly but most of these are the copyright of Gazza.

Golf

If the Romans had invented golf, they wouldn't have bothered with throwing the Christians to the lions. They would simply have given them a five-iron and a ball and let them suffer that way. Not only is golf just about the most frustrating way of spending an afternoon other than trying to play Scrabble with your blind granny, but the golf course is also a gladiatorial battleground where reputations are made and jobs are lost. It is the natural hunting place of the office yes man who will take care to give the boss a competitive game before managing to snatch defeat from the jaws of victory right at the death. He might achieve this by taking a putter off the tee on a par five ('I'm going for a low trajectory to counter the prevailing wind'), using a one wood to get out of a steep bunker ('It must have been next to the sand-wedge in my bag'), or putting out of bounds when only two feet from the hole ('These greens really are lightning fast'). And everybody retires happily to the 19th.

On the other hand, there is the fierce competitive element which arises out of a game between two young bucks. These contests have precious little to do with ability, but more with psychological warfare and cheating. There may be a very good reason why you want to beat your opponent at any cost. It could be the result of some slight – he may have slept with your girlfriend or, equally seriously, pinched your parking space. Or it could be a matter of envy – he may have once touched Philippa Forrester on the Circle Line, he could be the sole custodian of the keys to the office drinks cabinet, or he may just simply have a bigger todger than you. In these circumstances, you will undoubtedly need to resort to tactics as dubious as Bianca Butcher's dress sense in order to secure victory.

By far the most opportune moment to unnerve your opponent is when he's half-way through his backswing. At this point, he is utterly helpless, eyes firmly focused on the ball, so a sudden cough, sneeze or belch, a rustling of paper or a burst of whistling will destroy his concentration. Either he will abort the swing, risking grave personal injury, or he will drive the ball into the nearest woods. You may also wish to enter into conversation when he is at the top of his backswing. In truth, anything you say will have the desired effect but the following are particularly distracting:

- 'That's a really unusual stance you've got.'

- 'Watch out for those trees down the left.'

- 'Isn't that Concorde?'

- 'How do you manage to swing the club with a grip like that?'

- 'Look out!'

- 'If you don't mind my saying so, your legs should be further apart.' (Not to be used with lady golfers)

- 'What on earth's a pantomime horse doing on the green?'

- 'I've always admired your firm buttocks, Colin.'

- 'Did you know your wife's having an affair with your next door neighbour?'

If you are such an abysmal golfer that you need further help to win, then cheating is the answer. It worked for Maradona and it can work for you. The layout of the average golf course offers plenty of scope for subterfuge since a particularly bad player may not be seen by his opponent for a quarter of an hour at a time.

If you have hit your ball into the woods, race off in search of it, leaving your opponent trailing in your wake. Before he is in vision, either throw the ball out on to the fairway or, if you can't find your ball, take another from your bag and lob that out to safety. When he eventually appears, tell him you must have got a lucky bounce. Indeed it is a general rule in golf always to be first, either to your ball or your opponent's. For if your opponent has driven into the woods, he may have ended up with a fortunate lie which might mean him only losing one stroke. If you get there first, you can kick it much deeper into the undergrowth.

If his ball has clearly landed in the middle of the fairway, you may think there's not a lot you can do. Wrong. As you walk up to the ball, tread on it firmly, ramming it into the ground so that he'll need a stick of gelignite to reach the green. Alternatively, you can casually kick his ball into the nearest bunker and greet him with a cry of, 'Bad luck, old boy.'

Some bunkers have got less appealing faces than Keith Richards, in which case they can be a real bastard to get out of. Sometimes a tunnel seems the only way out. Should you find yourself in a really deep green-side bunker, ask your opponent to go forward to the green and tend the flag, just in case you should get lucky. That way, he won't be able to see you, allowing you to throw the ball up on to the green. But don't forget to toss up the obligatory shower of sand at the same time.

A game of golf is often won or lost on the green. Again, by being first on the scene, you can turn things to your advantage. You can either knock your opponent's ball further away from the hole, or if you are losing badly, into an adjacent water hazard. Another ruse is to mark your ball on the green, but then distract your opponent by engaging him in some meaningless conversation for 30 seconds or more, and replace the ball nearer to the hole, remembering to scoop up your marker at the same time.

Lady Golfers

Without doubt, the lady golfer is the most fearsome breed known to Man. A warrior race who craftily dress to make themselves appear several sizes larger than most women and therefore more imposing, they stalk the fairways in search of any male thought to be contravening the rule book. As a result of her prickly nature, the lady golfer is extremely easy to annoy.

Being in possession of male genitalia is invariably sufficient. Since there is more chance of Tom and Jerry existing in perfect harmony, there is not much point in pussyfooting around – you might as well go the whole hog. What's that Welsh proverb about being as well-hung for a sheep as a lamb? Some blokes have been known to resort to doing number twos in the hole as a nice little greeting for a ladies' foursomes, but we couldn't possibly condone that. However, you could try bonking your bird in a bunker. If a lady golfer catches you in the act, she will storm over with a face like thunder and demand: 'Are you members?' At this juncture, it is probably wise to resist any member jokes and beat a hasty retreat instead. If they're driving round in one of those golf buggies, let the hand-brake off when it's on a hill and watch them waddle off after it, trying to catch it before it tumbles into the lake.

The other thing about lady golfers is that they're so slow. Perhaps it's all that excess baggage they're carrying. If you're stuck behind them, you can waste a good hour of valuable drinking time while they line up their putts and practise their swings. You wouldn't mind if they took as much time with the Immac, and there's more chance of Dani Behr being voted Woman of the Year than there is of them waving you through. So you have to lump it, but if you're a reasonable player you can at least put the proverbial cat among the pigeons. Spray a few shots to land within 20 yards of them, getting progressively nearer each time. At first, you'll just get the Frosty the Snowman treatment, but by the third time, they'll march over, guns blazing, to deliver a verbal volley and maybe wrap a three iron round your head. You can either accept your punishment meekly, protesting that it was just a lucky shot, or, if you happen to have a Dobermann in your golf bag, you can encourage him to calm the situation.

In the Clubhouse

The game of golf thrives on social etiquette and nowhere is this more apparent than in the clubhouse. You've got to be pretty desperate to want a pint in a golf clubhouse. The prices are steep and the place is usually full of old buffers who look a nine iron away from rigor mortis. Most establishments have a strict dress code (no shorts, no jeans, no shirts unless they've got a silly motif with a golfer on the pocket and no sweaters unless they've got a diamond pattern and are endorsed by Nick Faldo or his lover). Some clubs won't allow you in unless you're wearing a tie although the rules rarely stipulate that it has to be around your neck. So tie it around your waist and see what sort of reaction you get.

8 MORE WAYS TO IRRITATE PEOPLE IN THE GOLF CLUBHOUSE

1. Say what a crap game golf is.
2. Say, 'I don't think much of the crumpet around here.' Some of them are probably married to it.
3. Call the barman 'John', as in 'Oi, John, two pints over here'. This insult is less effective if his name happens to be John, so it is best to check first.
4. Ask any of the members if they've ever seen *Eurotrash* and when they say no, describe it to them in graphic detail, particularly the story about the Italian lesbians and the model of the Leaning Tower of Pisa.
5. Tell them you think life insurance is a big con.
6. Complain because there are no kebabs on the menu.

7. Tell the barman, 'You need a few girlie calendars in here to liven the place up a bit.'

8. Say, 'Let's hope the Americans win the next Ryder Cup, eh?'

Cricket

The most unsociable thing you can do as an onlooker at a County Championship match is to go round waking up the other three spectators. All you will receive for your efforts are comments like, 'Is Compton out? Have the Germans surrendered?'

Therefore playing the game offers more scope for behaving badly, particularly when fielding – a seemingly timeless exercise which needs all the help it can get to make it interesting. Your captain will inevitably take the game far too seriously, in the belief that he is about to regain the Ashes rather than leading the Rose and Crown into a gentle knockabout against the Three Horseshoes followed by an almighty piss-up. For most club cricketers, the playing comes secondary to the drinking, but the captain tends to be the exception. He expects you to be concentrating on the play at all times, so the sight of you puffing away on a cigarette, making calls on your mobile phone, swigging from a can of lager, chatting up the girls at the boundary's edge or telling jokes to deep fine leg will drive him to distraction. All of this is much easier to do if you are stationed in the outfield, which is a bit like hiding away at the back of the class. If you are nearer to the wicket, you will find yourself subjected to closer scrutiny. That's not to say you can't have any fun. A favourite trick is to keep an orange in your pocket and when the ball comes your way, hold on to the ball but return the orange hard to the wicket-keeper. His natural instinct will be to catch it, the result being a horrible splattering sound and a messy pair of gloves. If you're bowling, you can try a similar ploy, delivering a nice juicy half-volley with a Cox's orange pippin. As the batsman is tempted into a full-blooded drive, he will get a nasty shock when the 'ball' disintegrates on contact, showering him in apple juice.

The other great pleasure to be derived from fielding close to the wicket is insulting the batsman. The Australians, who are very much pioneers in the world of behaving badly, have naturally enough turned this into an art form, known as 'sledging'. It operates on the principle that the greater the insult, the more likely the batsman is to be unsettled and therefore to surrender his wicket.

5 SUITABLE SUBJECTS FOR SLEDGING

1. The batsman's parentage – suggesting his parents could be Welsh.
2. The sexual appetite of the batsman's wife or girlfriend.
3. The ability of the batsman – or lack of it.
4. The size of the batsman's genitalia – or lack of it.
5. The relative merits of English and Australian lagers.

Rugby

Attending a rugby match for the first time is rather like going to the opera – there's a lot of frenetic action, but you haven't the faintest idea what's going on. Still, you can wile away the entire 80 minutes by asking the chap next to you to explain the offside rule. As with cricket, drinking is a major factor in rugby and it is compulsory to call in to the pub on the way to the match. With so many bladders to be emptied, you'd think the bogs at rugby grounds would be vast affairs, almost as big as the main stand. Instead they are so cramped you're never quite sure whose knob you're holding and you find yourself standing in a sea of piss. As an example of primitive behaviour, it ranks alongside the first day of Debenhams' winter sale. In a big crowd, there is absolutely no hope of getting to the bog and back without missing the entire match, but fortunately, since many rugby grounds are open to the elements, spectators tend to wrap up in large coats with ample pockets. So the solution is simple: you just piss in the pocket of the bloke in front. Having done so, it is probably advisable to move, just in case he reaches into his pocket for a mint imperial.

On a particularly cold day, you may have sought solace in a meat pie, but there are always the boring veggie bits to dispose of. You could try eating them, of course, but you can never be quite sure what they are so it's much better to flick them at the heads of the spectators lower down the terracing. Call me old fashioned, but there is something deeply satisfying about making a chunk of swede stick to a bloke's perm.

Drag Racing

All right if you like watching men run about in skirts and high heels.

Our House

BEHAVING BADLY AT HOME

The great thing about living in a place of your own is that you can do as you please. Parents are all very well, but they can be a bit restrictive. Living in your own pad, however, you can bring your mates back when you want, bring women back when you want and, God forbid, even forget to hang the tea-towel over the radiator. There's no need to worry about beer stains on the carpet or those strange sticky stains on the sofa – the ones you can't remember when they got there and off whom. In fact, they all help to give the place a sense of warmth, that lived-in feeling. And it doesn't matter that there's enough food on the kitchen floor to feed the Third World. Your mum will say proudly: 'You could eat off our kitchen floor.' Well with yours, it looks as if somebody has! Also you can decorate the place however you want – no wishy-washy magnolias or barleycorns, which are just white with A-levels. If you want to paint the whole flat black, you can. Besides, if you pick up a girl who's a coal miner it will make her feel at home.

Buying a place of your own is not something to be taken lightly. It is one of the most important decisions you will ever make and, as such, there are a number of factors which must be taken into consideration. These are:

- How far is it to the nearest pub? Any property more than four doors away from the nearest licensed premises is clearly unsuitable.

- Is there room for a bar in the lounge?

- Is there room for a pool table? This doesn't have to be in the lounge – it could even be in the bedroom. In fact, stick a mattress on top and it could serve a dual purpose.

- What are the neighbours like? You don't want to be stuck in a street full of wrinklies. They may be all right for organizing Neighbourhood Watch schemes, whist drives and modelling cardigans, but they suffer from a low tolerance level of really loud music at two in the morning. No, find an area with plenty of young blood, preferably female foreign-language students who, when you ask them for a cup of sugar, think you are asking them to take off their bra and panties.

- What is the view like? Is it just boring stuff like houses and trees or, if you press yourself at an angle of 47 degrees against the bedroom window, can you get an eyeful of said female foreign-language students going topless in next door's garden? Also, what's the view like from the kitchen? If you can see into other people's bedrooms, it will make heating spaghetti hoops all the more pleasurable. In fact you'll find you're never out of the kitchen with the prospect of more fanny than Johnny Cradock ever saw.

- What is the structure like? Are the walls so thin that you can hear every sigh and every groan of the couple next door's love-making? If so, snap it up at once.

Blokes often share when they first buy a place of their own. Whilst this arrangement creates more beer money, it can also be fraught with difficulties. Sharing a flat with the wrong bloke can be as bad as any marriage and you haven't even got the pleasure of the odd reconciliatory jump to look forward to. If you're naturally untidy, prone to washing up every alternate week, the last thing you want is a house-proud flat-mate who witters away like Simon off *EastEnders*. You might not mind too much at first, but his nagging and introduction of rotas will quickly wear you down. Similarly, if you're reasonably tidy about the house, you don't want to end up living with someone who boasts the national collection of half-eaten pizzas under his bed. There are also other factors to be taken into consideration when choosing a bloke to share with. Avoid any of the following:

- Someone who has a crush on you.

- Someone who spends an hour in the bathroom every morning.

- Someone who is better looking than you.

- A manic depressive.

- A pyromaniac.

- A psychopath.

- A teetotaller.

- A lay preacher.

- Someone who has featured on *Britain's Most Wanted*.

- Someone who invites sheep back to his place.

- The World Farting Champion.

- Someone who is £20,000 in debt.

- Someone who likes rap music.

Once you've moved in to your new place, you can start to think seriously about the decor. Between the full-size posters of Kate Bush circa 1980, Kim Wilde in her horny phase, Liz Hurley on all fours and Ulrika in bondage gear, you may need to add a dash of paint. The mood you are trying to create is that of the home of a Love God where the air positively crackles with sensual passion, so it might be an idea to visit a few brothels beforehand to pick up ideas for colour schemes. But remember that B&Q might not stock helmet purple.

The Lounge

The two most important items of furniture in a bloke's lounge are the sofa and the telly. If you play your cards right, your sofa will see more action over the years than a White House researcher. Your sofa harbours many secrets: on the one hand, it is a DNA database containing, as it does, the bodily fluids of most of the neighbourhood; on the other, it is a second larder concealing half-slices of pizza, lost noodles, errant crisps and squashed Maltesers. It is possible to enjoy a sumptuous three-course meal from the contents of a particularly well-used sofa. People have been known to find a whole chicken and an Italian waiter down the side of their sofa. And thirdly, it provides a home for thousands of species of insect – mites, spiders, colonies of wood lice, all feasting off your anchovy topping.

Indeed your average sofa will have more bugs than MI5. It may even house the odd rodent, too.

It is as a casting couch, however, that the sofa comes in most useful – when the sight of Pippa Greenwood spraying her woolly aphids on *Gardeners' World* drives you to such heights of ecstasy that you and your girlfriend have to do it there and then. Position yourself so that you can still see Pippa squeezing the nozzle and the joy will be unsurpassable.

When your mates come round, your sofa will come into its own as a landing mat. After a few cans, you'll all want to be trying a flying vault over the arm of the sofa, 2.4 difficulty with twist and pike, to land face up on the far cushion. The winner earns five minutes alone in the loo with a photo of Olga Korbut in her leotard. The loser gets five minutes alone in the loo with a photo of a Russian weightlifter in her leotard.

If one of your mates starts to doze off as a result of E.L.I. (Excessive Lager Intake), turn the volume on the telly up full blast to shock him out of his lethargy. If he dozes off with his mouth open, start lobbing in peanuts. If he starts to doze off during a Swedish porno video, find a new mate.

The worst thing that can happen to your lounge is for your girlfriend to move in. Now in principle there's nothing wrong with that – you'll have sex on tap and someone to do all the washing, ironing and cooking – but you'll also find that overnight, all your CDs will be re-arranged into alphabetical order, your smelly trainers will be deposited in the hall, an ashtray will be introduced to stop you stubbing out your fag ends on the carpet, a 'no-gobbing-in-the-waste-paper-basket' rule will be implemented, the sofa will be adorned with chintz cushions and the front window will have curtains which meet in the middle. Life will never be the same again.

The Kitchen

The only item of importance in the modern kitchen is the fridge. This should be crammed at all times with cans of nicely chilled lager, for there is scarcely an event in life which can not be enriched by a decent can of the golden nectar. Indeed, just about the only occasion when you can't drink lager is when you're asleep... unless you've got a mate who's a doctor and who can fit you up with an intravenous drip of Carling Black Label.

13 UNDERRATED OCCASIONS FOR SWIGGING A CAN OF LAGER

1. As your aunt's coffin is being lowered into the ground.
2. On your first day at school.
3. While being breathalysed by the police.
4. Watching your partner give birth.
5. To accompany smoked salmon.
6. On the bog.
7. As you take your marriage vows.
8. At a job interview.
9. In the shower.
10. During sexual intercourse.
11. Being introduced to the vicar.
12. During your driving test.
13. At an Alcoholics' Anonymous meeting.

It is a widely recognized fact that men are better cooks than women. Look at all the top chefs – they're all men. OK, so Delia hasn't done too badly, but one swallow doesn't make a belch, as they say. It's just that men have got so many other things to occupy their lives that they simply haven't got time to do the cooking as well. Whereas women, all they do is produce the odd baby, watch the lunchtime edition of *Home and Away* and then they're at a loose end. They can't hold their drink, they don't appreciate porno movies, they know naff all about football, so they might as well cook something. And what do they do? They cook the same things week after week, year after year. In most households, you can tell what day of the week it is by what's on the dinner table. If it's sausage and mash, it must be Monday.

When lads do find the time to cook, they don't opt for the boringly conventional. They slip their mate's socks in the microwave or come up with truly inventive recipes. Here are a few taken from the sort of foodstuffs lying around any lad's kitchen.

- Mouldy cheese in a nice lager sauce.

- Spaghetti hoops *tartare* (uncooked spaghetti hoops).

- Corn flakes *au gratin* (corn flakes with the mouldy cheese sprinkled on top).

- Instant Noodle Surprise (it's edible).

- Cereal Italienne (corn flakes with the spaghetti hoops).

- Spaghetti hoops *au chocolat* (spaghetti hoops with a Kit-Kat on top).

- Spaghetti *a la Carlsberg* (self-explanatory).

A LAD'S TOP-SIX COOKERY TIPS

1. Never eat anything that looks as if it might be good for you. It will always taste foul.

2. Never decide on any meal that requires more than five minutes' preparation (this is particularly relevant now that the pubs are open all day).

3. If it doesn't go with lager, it's not even worth thinking about.

4. Avoid vegetables at all costs.

5. Try it out on a neighbour's dog or your mate first – just in case.

6. Pop down to the local takeaway. Remember, your custom is vital. Without it, all the kebab farmers in under-developed countries would go bust.

Whilst men are often accomplished cooks, they are useless at washing-up. They simply have no interest in it – rather like sewing, leg-waxing or visiting relatives for Sunday tea. Consequently, they leave it to pile up for weeks on end, in the process allowing coffee mugs to develop spores which would be of immense fascination to David Bellamy. The hope is that a passing girl will eventually take pity on them and do the lot in one fell swoop.

While you're in the kitchen, bet your mate a quid that he can't sing "Save Your Kisses For Me" while balancing a glass of water on each hand. He'll jump at the chance, even when you point out that the glasses must be placed on the backs of his hands. As he stands there arms outstretched, recapturing Brotherhood of Man's finest hour, you simply walk out and go to the pub, leaving him stranded and with no way of putting down the glasses.

The Bathroom

The most important thing in the bathroom is to keep the inside of the toilet bowl relatively clean. After all, it's the view you and your mates will see most often. What you don't want to see when you chuck up are bits of tomato and diced carrot left over from the previous night's excesses.

Generally speaking, blokes spend a lot of time on the loo. After a hot curry, it can be as much as every ten minutes. It's a place for contemplation, meditation and relaxation, a haven from the pressures of the outside world. The only time it ceases to be relaxing is when you forget to bolt the door and your mate nips in and, barking like the Andrex puppy and swipes the toilet roll. Still, you'll get your revenge by placing a sheet of clingfilm over the bowl in readiness for the next time he goes for a piss.

Brown may be a pretty dreary colour, but it looks good on the walls of a bathroom, especially if you're a curry-lover. There's no sense in creating unnecessary work.

To shower or to bath? That is one of the great dilemmas facing mankind as we approach the millennium. New men lean towards a shower because it is much quicker and allows them to get on with the ironing or to get to their flower-arranging class. But we traditionalists prefer a good long soak in the bath, if only because it takes us back to our childhood where most of us are still firmly – and happily – rooted. First, it was your rubber duck and then you graduated to ships with little holes in the side so that when you filled it up with bath water, it sank. It is thought that the *Titanic* was modelled on these lines. In fact, it may well have been in the bath that you put your fast-developing todger to its first gainful use by casting it as the iceberg which sank the *Titanic*. Now that you have grown up into a mature adult, you enjoy nothing more than creating your own jacuzzi in the bath, courtesy of a few healthy farts. Watching the bubbles rise to the surface continues to be a source of wonderment, and the smell is always more pungent – something to bottle for posterity. A bath-time pursuit which should be avoided, however, is one involving any part of your anatomy and the plughole. Apart from anything else, it takes a lot of explaining in casualty.

Unless there is a specific invitation for you to join them in a sea of foam, girls tend to lock the door when having a bath, but men are less reserved. So if you share a flat with a mate, a carefully planned bath-time raid means that you can attack at a time when he is powerless to fight back.

6 THINGS TO DO TO YOUR FLAT-MATE WHILE HE IS IN THE BATH

1. Tip a bucket of freezing cold water over him.
2. Remove all the towels.
3. Grab his clothes and throw them out of the window.
4. Pour vinegar into his bath water. He'll come out stinking like a pickled onion.
5. Empty into the bath the tank containing his pet piranha.
6. Throw the electric heater into the bath (this is only if you're looking for a new flat-mate or want to live in prison).

But remember, no matter how much you enjoy a bath, don't overdo it. Think of the constant need for world water conservation and the damage that too many baths can do to your skin. You don't want to end up old and wrinkly like Albert Steptoe. Also, it's not easy to perform straight after a hot bath, so limit your ablutions – once a fortnight should be enough to remove the top layer of grime.

The Bedroom

Depending on your luck, the bedroom can either be the busiest or the loneliest room in the flat. The first aim of any relationship is to lure the girl into your bedroom. Whereas in most cases, your natural charm should be enough to make her drop them the moment she steps over the threshold, in other instances you may need to dangle a metaphorical carrot – not that you're suggesting in any way that she resembles a donkey, although it's a comparison you yourself would be quite flattered by. It's just a means of enticing her towards the bedroom. So always keep your most interesting exhibits in the bedroom so that when she asks to see them, you can reply in a matter-of-fact way, 'OK, they're in the bedroom. Come through.' These exhibits don't even have to be something you're remotely interested in, just as long as they are innocent and have a certain appeal to women, things such as:

- A collection of decorative hair slides.

- A collection of wild flower tea-towels.

- A scale model of the Taj Mahal, made out of plasticine.

- Doilies through the ages.

- A collection of photos of seal pups.

On the other hand, some collections are definitely inadvisable for this purpose. They include:

- A collection of girlie magazines.

- A collection of ladies' underwear.

- A scale model of Ulrika Jonsson, made out of plasticine and bits of a Brillo pad.

- A collection of empty peanut butter jars.

- A collection of beer mats.

- A collection of erotically shaped vegetables.

- A collection of photos of seal pups being clubbed to death.

- A collection of inflatable dolls.

- A platter of wet fish.

- A collection of medieval torture implements.

- A collection of bottles of chloroform.

It does no harm to leave a packet of condoms on your bedside table. She's not to know that you're sex-mad; she'll think you're just a caring guy who is aware of the need to take precautions.

Mates (the friends not the condoms) are supposed to stick together. They are meant to support each other through thick and thin, but one situation guaranteed to put a strain on any friendship is when your flat-mate is shagging a girl in the next room while you're sitting in bed with nothing for company but a well-thumbed copy of *Knave*. At times like this, as you listen to his bed-springs taking a terrible pounding and hear more cries of 'Oh God' than on the Christmas Eve *Songs of Praise* special, it is hard not to feel just a touch envious.

Suddenly you find yourself tempted to sabotage his 15 minutes of fame, justifying your actions by the knowledge that if the positions were reversed, he would do exactly the same to you. Among the options open to you are:

• Playing music at full volume.

• Knocking on his door and asking whether you can borrow a CD.

• Practising the cello.

• Ringing him on the mobile phone he keeps next to his bed.

• Launching yourself into a fake coughing fit.

• Knocking on his door and asking him whether he'd mind keeping the noise down – you're trying to get some sleep.

• Start drilling holes in the wall in readiness for putting up that shelf you've been meaning to get round to for a year.

• Doing animal impressions.

If none of these measures put the pair of them off, you'll just have to turn the other cheek, go to sleep and get your revenge when he climbs into his bed the following night. A long-standing form of bed sabotage is the apple pie bed, a contraption which is so impenetrable that the frustrated would-be occupant will end up sleeping on top of the bed rather than in it. Start by tucking in the bottom sheet all around the bed and then add the top sheet, tucking it in at the top and the upper sides. Then put the pillow on top of the top sheet before folding the top sheet back from the bottom of the bed so that it covers the pillow. Finally, fold back the top sheet to reveal the pillow, add blankets and tuck everything firmly in place. From the outside, the top sheet will look like two sheets, but when your mate tries to climb in, he'll find there is nowhere for his legs. Or you could try slipping something unwelcome into his bed. Among the things he won't want to find when he gets into bed are:

- A leaking hot water bottle.

- A live alligator.

- Boy George.

- A mouse trap.

- Blancmange.

- A ferret.

- A dozen sprigs of holly.

- A scorpion.

- His ex-girlfriend armed with a bread knife.

The Garden

As a rule, lads can't be bothered with gardening. The only time they are prepared to get muddy is playing football or in the course of an alfresco leg-over. You could try making an anonymous phone call to the police to report that there is a body buried in your garden. It will save you having to dig it, but if you get found out, it will land you with a charge of wasting police time. Anyway gardens need not be mountains of hard work and on hot summer evenings, they are the perfect settings for barbecues and scantily clad girls. The majority of gardeners are civilized, well-behaved individuals which allows you to become the exception.

7 WAYS OF BEHAVING BADLY IN THE GARDEN

1. Throw all your weeds over the fence into the garden next door.

2. Light a bonfire as soon as the woman next door hangs out her washing.

3. Erect a display of flashing fairy lights, positioning them so that they reflect in your neighbour's window all night.

4. Cavort around stark naked, but be careful when approaching rose bushes, cutting the edges of the lawn with shears or cooking sausages on the barbecue.

5. Plant a hedge of *Cupressus leylandii* close to your neighbour's window. In a few years, it will be so dark he'll think he's living in a cave.

6. Creep into next door's garden in the dead of night and start moving their garden gnomes around. Keep doing this every week or so until your neighbours are thoroughly perplexed. Get more daring as you go along, placing the little chaps in compromising positions with each other or performing indecent acts with the stone

frog, thus giving a new meaning to 'having a frog in
your throat'.

7. Decide to mow your lawn at two o'clock in the morning.

First Cut is the Deepest

AT THE HAIRDRESSER

With all this stuff about childhood traumas having a profound effect on your adult life, it's a wonder blokes go anywhere near a hairdresser's. For your first ten years on this earth – more, if you've got callous parents – you are sent to some back-street barber where a bloke with a razor that looks as if it was once used for shearing sheep scalps you to within a quarter of an inch of your life. You emerge looking like a prisoner of war and with enough Brylcreem on what's left of your hair to make you keep sliding off the pillow when you go to bed at night. So when you reach your teenage years and choose your own coiffeur, it is hardly surprizing that you steer well clear of anyone likely to be a direct descendant of Sweeney Todd.

Instead you opt for a place with girl stylists, hoping that her map of Tasmania will brush against you at some point or that you will be able to make eye contact with her cleavage as she does round your ears. But you always end up with some bird who's going through what can only be described as an experimental hair phase. If she wants to look like Ken Dodd, fine, but you're not sure you want to entrust your locks to someone with such dodgy taste. The other disappointments are always the style photos on the wall. Blokes don't want to gaze at pictures of immaculately groomed smoothies who appear to have walked straight out of knitting patterns, just in case we come out looking like that. If we must study hair, we want it to be girlie hair, preferably of the short and curly variety.

When you're stuck in the chair, you're in the passive position. Your hands are tucked away under the cape and anyway, any attempt at intimate touchy-feely will probably result in the top of your ear being sliced off. You can test the water by asking for a cut and blow job and when she says, 'You mean blow dry?', say 'Oh, has Natalie left then?' But otherwise all you can do is listen to her inane questions.

Hairdressers are not exactly renowned for their Jeremy Paxman-type interrogation. It is a well-known fact that they only have two questions in their repertoire – 'Doing anything nice for the weekend?' (this can be asked even on a Monday) and 'Been away on holiday yet?' If you're there in the middle of the morning, they may choose to throw in a supplementary 'Not working today then?', but this, rather like giving you a decent haircut, is left very much to their discretion. You could try feigning outrage at this last question, claiming that you've been unemployed for three years and that your life has been devastated by your failure to land a job, but the chances are that she won't listen to your reply and will just say, 'Oh, that's nice.'

In view of the fact that she is programmed not to hear a word you say, you might as well come up with something challenging. So when she asks what you've got planned for the weekend, tell her one – or indeed all – of the following:

- I'm running off to Mustique with Cameron Diaz.

- I'm going to assassinate Little Jimmy Osmond and systematically work my way through every child star who's ever had a top-20 hit.

- I'm going to sail solo around the world in a large saucepan.

- I'm going to liberate all of the world's mistreated potatoes. Vegetarians don't realize that King Edwards have feelings too, you know.

- I'm going to wash that man right out of my hair.

- I'm going to ask you to marry me.

Please Mr Postman

MALICE THROUGH THE LETTER-BOX

Among the simplest methods of baffling one of your mates is to fill in those coupons you get in newspapers which advertise all sorts of products from potions guaranteed to combat hair loss (usually promoted by a sporting personality who still looks remarkably short in the follicle department) to another cream (or maybe the same one) designed to tackle impotence. You just fill in his name and address and wait for him to receive a stack of junk mail. And the great thing about these companies is that once he's on their mailing list, they'll carry on besieging him with brochures for years to come. So he'll still be getting impotence leaflets when he's a father of four. But mail hoaxes are even more effective (for effective, read embarrassing) if the offending literature is opened by somebody else – such as his wife or mother, or a nosy neighbour.

If you've got the technology, you can compose your own headed notepaper from a fictional firm, but even if you just use plain paper, your letter can still be convincing as long you set it out neatly. Something along these lines should serve to create an air of anger and suspicion in your mate's home.

Loan-U-Like Finance Co.

Dear Mrs Rogers,

Despite repeated requests for your husband to repay an outstanding loan of £5,000, taken out on 12 January 1997, he has so far failed to do so. The interest on this loan now totals an additional £7,497.44, making a total owed to us of £12,497.44. If we do not receive an instalment of at least £1,000.00 by this Friday (the 20th), we shall be seeking a court order, as a result of which you will almost certainly be liable to forfeit your home and possessions. Have a nice day.

Yours sincerely,

Or perhaps...

Marianne's Private Clinic

Dear Mrs Rogers,

As you probably know, your husband came to this clinic recently to undergo tests for a wide range of sexual complaints. You probably also know that last week we sent him the results which showed that he tested positive for gonorrhoea. Therefore I am writing to remind you that under no circumstances should you attempt sexual intercourse with your husband for a period of at least six months until we have been able to treat the disease effectively.

Yours sincerely,

Other suitably embarrassing tricks include:

- Sending a letter to your mate from a private investigator revealing that, in the course of his work on a case, he has regularly seen your mate's wife with a married man.

- Wrap half a dozen explicit girlie magazines in a plain brown package and tear the package so that the title and part of the front cover are clearly visible. Then, when you know your mate isn't at home, call on the spinster who lives next door to him and ask her whether she would mind passing the parcel on to him.

- Arrange for a stair-lift to be delivered to your mate's home on a free trial.

- Send a letter to your mate's wife from a girl claiming to be the mother of his secret love-child and complaining that he has suddenly stopped making maintenance payments.

- Send a letter to your mate from a travel company, confirming the booking of him and his secretary in a double room at a two-star hotel in Minehead for a week at the end of July. But address the envelope to his wife by mistake so that she opens it.

- Send a letter from a private nursing home to your mate's mother, stating that her son has made inquiries about having her put in a home. Since she is only 60 and in the best of health, this will come as a nasty shock to her.

- Send your mate a letter from his local pub, stating that he has been banned for unruly behaviour.

- Send an irate letter to your mate's wife from a wronged husband claiming that their respective spouses are having an affair.

- Send a letter to your mate from the council, informing him that the highways planning committee have approved the construction of a new six-lane motorway to run within 20 yards of his house.

- Write a letter to your mate from a girl you know he once slept with, disclosing that she is pregnant and is certain that he is the father.

- Book your mate and his girlfriend on a Saga coach tour to Worthing.

Where the Streets Have No Name

OUT AND ABOUT

Why is it that whenever you're a visitor to a strange town somebody always comes up and asks you for directions? It can be mildly irritating if you're in a hurry or trying to dodge the patches of pavement pizza. So instead of admitting that you don't know your way around either, pretend that you know every inch of the city and send the lost soul off on a wild goose chase involving a mile walk, an Underground journey and two bus rides. If somebody comes up and asks you the way in your own town, give them detailed instructions which, after a good half-hour's walk, will take them full circle. By that time, of course, you will have long gone. Other people will stop you in the street to ask you the time, but there are a number of deterrents you can employ on this and other occasions:

- Pretend to be deaf and ask your inquisitor to speak up a little. When they repeat the request, protest that you still can't hear and tell them to speak louder. Carry on like this until they are shouting at the top of their voice. If they still refuse to give up, walk away muttering something about having to get batteries for your hearing aid.

- Pretend to be a foreign visitor, gesturing something along the lines of 'No speaka Englasi'.

- Sway from side to side, pretending to be so drunk that you are about to throw up all over them. They'll quickly find someone else to ask.

- If someone asks you for directions, tell them you're sorry but you only got out of prison that morning after serving 15 years for the murder of an innocent passer-by. Unless the person asking you is an ex-con or Lord Longford, he will quickly search for a less dangerous alternative.

- When somebody asks you a simple question such as the time, immediately fly into a manic rage. 'Questions, questions, that's all I ever get! I don't want to answer any more questions! I hear voices, you know. And they keep asking me questions. All the time. All day and all night. It's driving me insane, at least that's what the doctors think. I need help not questions.' And then storm off.

- As you are asked for the time, turn the tables and ask your questioner for 10p for a cup of tea. For some reason, this only seems to work if you've got a mangy dog with you.

- Break down in floods of tears. 'I'm sorry. I'm sorry. But my girlfriend left me last night. She ran off with my best friend. Cleaned me out, she did. Took everything. Five years we'd been together. I'd given her everything she'd ever wanted and then she treats me like this. I don't know how I'm going to get through the day. My world is so empty without her. A drink would help but she took my wallet, my credit card, the lot, even my signed photos of Wallace and Gromit. I've got nothing except the clothes I'm standing in.' Continue sobbing uncontrollably and with any luck, instead of having to tell him the time, he'll give you the money for a pint. Or you could be unlucky and find that he's a social worker who'll direct you to the nearest night shelter.

• If you're with a mate when somebody asks you the way, the pair of you can launch into a mock argument as to the best directions. You say one way, he says the other and neither of you will agree that the other is right. Make the row become progressively more heated until, to the acute embarrassment of the onlooker, you actually come to blows. At that, he'll either slink away or try to act as peacemaker, in which case both of you can tell him to mind his own business and sod off.

The one inquiry you do want to encourage is when someone asks you where the nearest pub is. Offer to take them in person and, once inside, tell them you'll have a pint. You deserve a free drink for your help.

In the Queue

Queuing is a great British institution. It is a well-known fact that we queue for almost anything, but it is a popular misconception that we actually enjoy queuing. On the contrary, we hate it and moan like hell when the queue we're in is moving slower than the M25 in rush hour. Most of our queuing is done at places like the bank or the post office and there are a variety of reasons why your queue might be delayed:

• A little old lady wants to change her life savings into escudos.

- A woman with three screaming toddlers – Wayne, Jason and Darren – has buried her cheque book at the bottom of her shopping bag beneath an economy pack of disposable nappies, 20 packets of Marlboro, 16 cans of lager, five tins of dog food and a can of Libby's fruit cocktail.

- Although there are six cashier windows, bank rules seem to dictate that no more than one shall be open at any given time.

- The cashier is stupefyingly slow because she has to wait for her nail varnish to dry.

- The bank is being robbed.

Fortunately there are ways of getting to the head of a queue.

4 WAYS TO MAKE A QUEUE VANISH BEFORE YOUR VERY EYES

1. Sneeze violently and wipe an imaginary lump of snot off the shoulder of the person in front. They will quickly decide to come back later rather than be infected with your germs. Repeat along the line until you reach the front.
2. Save your finest farts for the queue. The odour will have the same effect on the people in front of you as Domestos does on 99 per cent of household germs.
3. Stick your fingers down your throat and chuck up over the people in front, landing lumps over as many bodies as possible. The stink alone will persuade them to

leave and come back another day.

4. Shout: 'Everybody on the floor. This is a raid.' As they hurl themselves to the ground, you can walk calmly to the window and get served.

Baggy Trousers

THE CLOTHES SHOW

Clothes are meant to be worn. It's an indisputable fact – that is definitely what they were designed for. For instance, if a pair of jeans was designed to hold water, presumably the inventor wouldn't have added legs with holes at the end. And if a shirt was intended to cook frozen lasagne in three minutes, why the sleeves? So why does anyone need a wardrobe full of clothes when you can only wear one lot at a time? Clothes should be like cars. You wear them into the ground every day and then get rid of them. You don't see people with a different car for each day of the week, do you? Well, not unless you live in Weybridge. Girls will have as many as eight pairs of near-identical shoes. Ask them why they've got so many and they'll tell you that the first pair pinch their toes; the second pair rub their heels; the third pair leak when it rains; the heels are too high on the fourth pair; the fifth pair don't really go with any of her skirts and anyway are too wide; the sixth pair don't look right with jeans and are too narrow; the seventh pair rub that bone on the side of her foot; and the eighth pair are really comfortable and look good with anything. So why not just have the one comfortable pair and give the rest to Imelda Marcos?

In contrast, men's wardrobes are much more spartan affairs. In fact, their wardrobes are usually full of old football programmes, magazines they don't want their mums to see when she visits and old pizza cartons. Clothes are crammed in a cardboard box on the floor, apart, that is, from the sweater with a giant penguin on the front that Great Aunt Hermione knitted you last Christmas, the sweater she knitted for your birthday (where one sleeve is four inches longer than the other) and the sports shirt your parents bought you in a dirty shade of camel. These are all in a black plastic bag bound for charity. In truth, your everyday clothes would be better off being sent to the Antiques Roadshow. Your trainers, as black on the inside as out, have seen you through seven girlfriends, one fiancæe, two paternity suits, a night in a police cell, nine holidays in Ibiza and three changes of job, your jeans have survived three Prime Ministers, five World Cups and two wars, while your sweatshirt is expecting a telegram from the Queen any day, having made it to 100 in sweatshirt years. Girls are puzzled as to how your sweatshirt lasts so long: the answer is simple – it's only ever been washed once.

Your trainers have become local celebrities. In the pub, they reckon they can smell your footwear coming a good minute and a half before you walk through the door. This notoriety means that you have to be extremely careful (or not) about leaving them lying around.

9 PLACES NOT TO LEAVE YOUR SMELLY TRAINERS

1. In the kitchen.

2. In the bathroom.

3. In anyone else's bedroom.

4. In your parents' lounge, especially during a silver wedding celebration.

5. At Buckingham Palace.

6. In Dolcis.

7. On the perfume counter in Boots.

8. On a table at Burger King.

9. Under the nose of anyone not suffering from a heavy cold.

Even the toughest trainers can't live for ever. Eventually there will come a time for a fond farewell, but rather than consign them to that great shoe rack in the sky, think of alternative uses for them.

FIVE USES FOR AN OLD PAIR OF TRAINERS

1. As a pot for growing hyacinths in.

2. As a decorative ornament.

3. As a dog bowl.

4. As a Christmas stocking, crammed full of satsumas, peanuts and chocolate.

5. As a spare drinking mug when all the others have been broken.

Although most lads' fashion statements are more like a stutter, there are certain rules to obey unless you want to find yourself carted away by the fashion police. The most basic is that there is no occasion designed by Man which could ever warrant your wearing a shell suit. At its best, on a slim babe, a shell suit manages to camouflage all the lovely curvy bits; at its worst, it looks like something Richard Branson would try to fly around the world. As a fashion statement, a shell suit says three things: 'I'm sad,' 'My mum still dresses me,' and 'I go to car boot sales.'

15 RULES OF FASHION

1. Never iron your jeans.
2. Don't attempt to remove any telltale stains from your jeans – it gives them character.
3. Never change your pants more than twice a week.
4. Never change your socks more than once a week.
5. If your socks get a hole in them, wear them until it becomes painful and then chuck them out. On no account, darn them. Darning socks went out in the Sixties.
6. Show off your holy socks to your boss. It will prove to him that you're not interested in material wealth, but that you could do with a pay rise.
7. Never wear colours which are meant to go together.
8. Never wear clothes of all one colour, unless it's black and you're a burglar.
9. Avoid tartan, unless you want someone to think you're a former member of the Bay City Rollers.

10. Avoid checked shirts, unless you want anyone to think you're American.

11. Avoid lime green, unless you want to look like an Opal fruit.

12. Never wear pink, unless you intend going out alone on Hampstead Heath at night.

13. Never let your girlfriend buy anything with a leopard-skin print, unless you want to be seen going out with something that looks like Bet Lynch.

14. Never buy your girlfriend anything that doesn't give you an instant hard-on.

15. Wear odd socks – it will make you a talking point.

Where would we be without Americans? OK, you've got to have someone to laugh at, but we must also be grateful for some of the inventions which they have given the world – fast food, Meg Ryan and T-shirts. The T-shirt is a wonderfully versatile garment with a slogan to fit every occasion. However, some slogans are best kept for the pub or male company.

12 T-SHIRT SLOGANS LIKELY TO OFFEND A PROSPECTIVE MOTHER-IN-LAW

1. Mother Fucker.

2. Hi, You Fat Old Bag.

3. The Euthanasia Society.

4. Save Water, Bath with a Friend.

5. Rapist.

6. Don't Eat a Joint, Smoke One.

7. A Shag a Day Keeps the Doctor Away.

8. Never Mind the Bollocks.

9. Adolf Hitler's European Tour, 1939.

10. Make Prostitution Legal.

11. The Devil in Disguise.

12. Sheep Make Great Pets but Even Better Lovers – Slam in the Lamb.

Men don't care much for dressing up – unless they're on the pull. We'd quite happily go to our own wedding in a T-shirt and jeans, but there are some occasions when we have to make an effort, such as for a job interview.

11 CLOTHES FOR A MAN NOT TO WEAR AT AN INTERVIEW FOR AN OFFICE JOB

1. Camouflage combat jacket and trousers.

2. A pair of swimming trunks.

3. A T-shirt bearing the slogan: Power to the Workers.

4. The national costume of Denmark.

5. Scuba diving gear.

6. Bondage gear.

7. A Millwall replica shirt.

8. A sou'wester and oilskins.

9. A satin jump-suit.

10. A Donald Duck costume.

11. A floral dress.

Is (the) Vic There?

AS AN EXTRA ON *EASTENDERS*

You met a bloke in the pub the other night who reckoned he knew everyone in showbusiness. He claimed he was on first-name terms with Zoe Ball, Chris Evans, Sam Fox, as well as all the other stars. You and your mates thought he was a typical flash git, full of blarney and bluster, out to impress. There had been loads of them over the past few months: the bloke who reckoned Lord Lucan was staying at his house until two nights ago, the chap who insisted that Shergar was alive and well and grazing in a field just outside Hemel Hempstead; and the guy who said his dad had the crew of the *Marie Celeste* round for dinner. So you told him to put his money where his mouth was, but he couldn't insert a tenner up his backside. However he was adamant that his contacts book stretched to a second page and promised that he'd pull a few strings, call in a few favours and, within a week, you'd be appearing on television. You were still sceptical. Your mates reckoned you'd be the twat who always pulls funny faces behind John McCririck on Channel 4 racing, the bloke in the audience subjected to the electric cattle-prod treatment for not laughing at *Noel's House Party*, or the stroppy sheep on *One Man And His Dog*. Instead you learn that he's fixed you up with a walk-on part in *EastEnders*.

It's your moment of stardom, the chance of a lifetime. Unlike the greatest-ever Super Sofa Showroom sale which must end Sunday, it's a never-to-be-repeated offer. You're determined to enjoy yourself, no matter what.

22 WAYS OF UPSETTING PEOPLE ON THE SET ON *EASTENDERS*

1. Tell the cast you much prefer *Coronation Street*.
2. Wave to the camera half-way through a long take.
3. Shout 'Hello, mum' half-way through a long take.
4. Shout 'Cut!' half-way through a long take.
5. Offer the director advice.
6. Make rabbit ears with your fingers when standing behind Grant Mitchell during a take.
7. Sit in one of the star's chairs.
8. Say: 'This acting game's dead easy, isn't it?'
9. Show one of the stars a scurrilous front-page story about them in that morning's paper which claims that their marriage is on the rocks and their character is about to be killed off. Add, 'Still you've got to laugh, haven't you?'
10. Fart loudly in the middle of a tender scene between Ricky and Bianca.
11. Even though your part only requires you to walk through the background clutching a bacon sandwich from the café, slip in the death scene from *Hamlet*.
12. Instead of strolling normally through your scene, goose-step.
13. Chuck a brick through the window of the Queen Vic, yelling, 'This is from Sharon.'
14. Say to a couple of long-standing cast members: 'Don't you think you're overpaid for what you have to do?'
15. Go up to one of the actors and say: 'I read somewhere that the rest of the cast hate you. Is that right?'

171

16. Tell Pat Butcher she could do with losing some weight.

17. Complain to Mark Fowler about the quality of his radishes. Then tell him to lighten up.

18. Stick a note on Ian Beale's back saying 'Prat'.

19. Ask Pauline Fowler whether she's a natural blonde – nudge, nudge.

20. Ask Barbara Windsor whether she would re-enact the bra scene from *Carry On Camping*, just for you in the bar of the Queen Vic.

21. Tell Phil Mitchell to stop mumbling.

22. Call Grant Mitchell a dome-headed poof.

Stuck in the Middle With You

IN A LIFT

With the possible exception of learning that Hughie Green was your natural father, being stuck in a lift is one of the most terrifying things you are ever likely to experience. The claustrophobia, the fear of never being rescued, the lack of oxygen... and, if you have company on your adventure, you can make matters considerably worse.

8 WAYS OF BEHAVING BADLY WHEN TRAPPED IN A LIFT

1. Begin telling blood-curdling horror stories.
2. Loosen your tie, start gasping for breath and pant: 'My God, it's claustrophobic in here.'
3. Tell everyone that you read a news story about a group of people trapped in a lift in Chicago. 'It was two weeks before they were discovered. Every one of them was dead and their bodies were crawling with maggots.'
4. Announce that you've read that, in situations like this, the only way for people to survive is to start eating each other. Eye up the neurotic-looking woman in the corner and say: 'We'll start with you.'
5. Chuck up all over the floor.

6. Reveal that you're the Budleigh Salterton Ripper.

7. Say that you need to lighten the load and that therefore two people must be hurled to almost certain death down the shaft. 'Are there are any lawyers, estate agents or double-glazing salesmen here?'

8. Recite some interesting statistics about death.

If there's just you and a girl trapped:

- Try it on, suggesting that she might as well die happy.

- Suggest making wild passionate love in the hope that the noise will attract rescuers.

- Say that you've read in a medical book that sex will raise your body temperature, making you more likely to survive the night.

- Suggest that if she takes off her bra, you might be able to use it as a foot stirrup to lever yourself up to the hatch in the top of the lift.

- Suggest that you both remove all of your clothes to make the lift lighter and therefore less likely to go crashing to the bottom of the shaft.

- If she's thirsty, offer her something to suck on.

Cigarettes and Alcohol

PUT THE HELL INTO HEALTH FARM

Of all the prizes they give away on *Family Fortunes*, the stay at the health farm is even less inspiring than the murder mystery weekend. They might as well give away a prize of being attacked by a man with a large stick. Surely the only place in society for a health farm is as a criminal deterrent – an alternative to a young offenders' institution – because nobody in their right mind would want to go to one voluntarily. So the only way you are ever likely to find yourself at a health farm is because you've made some refreshingly honest comment to your girlfriend that she could do with losing a couple of pounds. OK, she says, she'll have a weekend at a health farm. Great, you think, you'll have the place to yourself, but before you can put the word around about the party to end all parties, she announces that she wants you to come too. Horrified though you are by the prospect of losing your love handles, you are won round by her promise of non-stop deviant sex for the first two weeks after your return.

However, two days at a health farm can seem like a month at the dentist's, so you will need to find some way of easing the pain. The most obvious solution is to smuggle in bottles of Stella Artois, prime cuts of rump steak and packets of Rothmans, but for some inexplicable reason this doesn't always meet with the approval of the camp commandant who demands that you adhere to a strict diet of Trill. Still, as our local kebab house owner always says, there's more than one way to skin a cat.

7 WAYS OF UPSETTING THE REGIME AT A HEALTH FARM

1. Spread rumours about mad lettuce disease.
2. Recount the great corned beef scare of the 1960s, but change it to parsley.
3. Tell the fat woman on the sun lounge that the slices of cucumber over her eyes make her look like Chi-Chi.
4. Taunt the inmates with tales of juicy steaks and succulent lamb chops.
5. Pretend to have a cardiac arrest so that they don't put you on the rowing machine again.
6. Go on hunger strike for red meat.
7. Brandishing a courgette in a plastic bag, hold up the guards and make a bid for freedom.

You've Got A Friend

AT OTHER PEOPLE'S HOUSES

Unless you are a hermit or have the social graces of a warthog, you will undoubtedly be invited round to other people's houses, maybe to watch a video, have a few drinks and take part in a highly competitive game of Trivial Pursuit. If it's just your mate's flat, you don't have to worry too much about what you do and say – it will probably be as big a tip as yours, but if you suddenly find yourself operating on a higher social level (being invited round to the house of your mate's posh, married sister), you will need to tread carefully, not least on the carpet. Therefore if your opening line is likely to be, 'I love a nice deep shag,' think again.

Actions Which Might Prove Upsetting in Other People's Homes

In the Bathroom

- Don't bother putting the seat up.

- Leave behind a floater.

- Aim your piss at little marks on the side and around the rim of the bowl, thereby splashing all over the bath mat.

- Aim your piss firmly at the toilet freshener. The force of the jet will rebound spectacularly to all parts of the bathroom.

- Have a piss with your eyes shut to test how accurate your aim is. If you discover that you've sprayed all up the wall, try to do better next time.

- Try stopping and starting your wee. It can be uncomfortable and messy, but it can also prove an invaluable asset if ever you feel you're about to have 'an accident'.

- If the toilet seat is unstable and you're afraid of getting guillotined, piss in the wash basin instead.

- Wee in the pot plant in the corner to see how it copes with acid rain.

- Don't bother flushing the bog.

- Use up all the toilet paper, but don't tell anyone.

- Block the toilet with paper.

- Wrap all the toilet paper around your head and body and stagger downstairs as an Egyptian mummy.

- Use the last of the soap but don't bother mentioning it.

- Make no attempt to mask the smell with the can of handily placed air freshener.

- If you're staying overnight, don't let on that you've forgotten to pack your toothbrush. Use someone else's without telling them.

- Squeeze the toothpaste from the middle of the tube.

- Write 'I Love Laura' in toothpaste on the bathroom mirror.

- Squeeze a big whitehead in the bathroom mirror, but don't bother to wipe it off.

- Wipe your filthy hands on a clean white towel.

- Leave the taps running after washing your hands.

- Keep quiet about the fact that you've broken the blind.

- If you're having a bath and have managed to soak the towel, just leave it in a crumpled wet heap on the floor.

- Leave your navel fluff in a pile on the bath.

- In the bath, use someone's face flannel to wash your arse.

In the Kitchen

- After grabbing a can of lager, leave the fridge door open.

- Overcome by hunger, take a bite out of the cheese in the fridge.

- Sneak into the larder and swap all the food around. Put the salt in the flour container, the flour in the sugar jar and so on.

- Grab a couple of crackers from the larder, leaving a trail of crumbs across the kitchen floor.

179

In the Lounge

- Don't wipe your feet before setting foot on the new carpet. Instead leave a trail of muddy prints.

- Put your feet up on the arms of the new sofa.

- Shake your mate's can of lager so that when he opens it, the froth goes all over the carpet.

- Stand your wet glass on the expensive table without using a coaster, thus creating a nice ring.

- Leave your empty cans lying on the floor, dripping onto the carpet.

- Flick cigarette ash over the carpet instead of using the ashtrays provided.

- Feed the dog something guaranteed to make it sick over the carpet.

- Find some wax in your ears and flick on to the sofa or carpet.

- Stick your hand down your pants, say 'I wondered what happened to that peanut' and pop it in your mouth.

- Treat an expensive ornament as a target for balls of paper.

- Play with the remote control, channel hopping all evening.

- Swap around their music collection so that some of the

CDs are in the wrong case. Next time they put on Sheryl Crow, they'll hear Chas 'n' Dave instead.

In the Hall

- If you're left alone for a few minutes, reset the burglar alarm so that next time the owners come home, half of the local police force will be hot on their heels.

In the Bedroom

- Ferret through the lady of the house's knicker drawer, remembering to have a good sniff in case there's a pair she's had on earlier in the day.

- Have a flick through her wardrobe. You might find some sexy gear which will make you see her in a different light.

- Hide an egg under the pillow and wait for the crunch.

Verbal Criticism to Upset Your Hosts

Outside of the bedroom, there are seven areas in which upwardly mobile couples are particularly sensitive: she is sensitive about her cooking, her dress sense, the cleanliness of her house and her choice of decor; he is sensitive about his car, his DIY skills and his music collection. No woman wants to hear that she has the culinary expertise of King Alfred or wears dresses that would look better with guy ropes, while no man wants to be told that he has the do-it-yourself skills of Frank Spencer and Beethoven's ear for music. Still, being polite for the sake of it – even if you are a guest in somebody else's house – isn't doing them any favours. How can they ever hope to improve if they don't know they're doing anything wrong. No, sometimes you have to be cruel to be kind. A few home truths never hurt anybody.

To Her

- 'Isn't gravy supposed to move?'

- 'The last time I saw a liquid like this sauce, it had a paint brush in it.'

- 'Is this dog food?'

- 'You must have spent hours slaving in the kitchen over this – you really shouldn't have bothered.'

- 'Are you trying to poison us?'

- 'Is this supposed to taste of nothing?'

- 'Can I just say that was pigging awful?'

- 'My mum's got a dress like that.'

- 'You look like a movie star in that coat – Lassie springs to mind.'

- 'It's nice that you can get a wide range of clothes in such a big size.'

- 'You dress sensibly. At least looking like that there's no danger of anybody trying it on with you.'

- 'It's hard to think that you and Julia Roberts are the same species.'

- 'Is that a cobweb up there?'

- 'I have trouble keeping my place clean too.'

- 'Dust. It gets everywhere, doesn't it? You do it one week, then the next thing you know you've got a thick covering, just like you have here.'

- 'Interesting walls. That colour used to be really popular.'

- 'I couldn't live with that painting. It reminds me of puke.'

- 'It's amazing what you can get from MFI.'

- 'Those ornaments could be worth a bob or two. Cheap tack's all the rage these days.'

To Him

- 'Whose is that rust bucket on the drive?'

- 'That's not a car – a Flymo's got more power than one of those.'

- 'That shelf doesn't look straight.'

- 'You should have got a professional in to do the decorating. I can let you have the name of a bloke I know.'

- 'You don't like Dire Straits! That's so middle class!'

- 'Haven't you got any decent music?'

The Dinner Party

Ever since Jesus invited a few mates round for the Last Supper, people have been obsessed with throwing dinner parties. Why? It's just a heap of allegedly nutritious home-cooked food (in other words nothing tasty), often of dubious Eastern European origin, which, when piled on a plate, looks like a cow's just dumped its load. And to think you could be having something that's really good for you, like a kebab or a vindaloo. And instead of being out with your mates, you end up having to listen to some plonker whose talk is so small it's in danger of disappearing altogether. And what does he insist on talking about? His precious job, his company car, his pension scheme, why Brazilian accountants find it difficult to settle in Teesside practices. You really have to work hard to get the conversation round to the clitoris.

The redeeming feature of dinner parties should be that the booze is free (except for the obligatory cheapest-bottle-in-the-shop-which-could-strip-the-plaque-off-your-teeth that you bring with you), but even then it's all wine. Now there's nothing wrong with a glass of good wine, provided it's been preceded by at least half-a-dozen lagers, but wine by itself is so... poncey. Hosts say things like, 'This wine complements the chicken,' and you think, 'That's funny, I haven't heard the wine say a word. Not once have I heard it say, "You're the nicest-looking chicken I've ever seen, with the best set of giblets."' No, all things considered, dinner parties should be treated like the plague.

8 EXCUSES FOR GETTING OUT OF A DINNER PARTY

1. You've got to cut your toe nails that night.
2. You've had a better offer from the church flower arranging society.
3. You're allergic to accountants.
4. You're allergic to her cooking.
5. You've got a low boredom threshold.
6. You'd better stay in just in case your neighbour spontaneously combusts and needs your help.
7. You're frightened of going out because you've heard that the Surrey Puma is on the loose again.
8. You don't want to miss *Panorama*.

If you can't find any way of getting out of the dinner party – or, more likely, you've been told a former Miss Doncaster is going to be there – there are certain rules of etiquette which should be followed. Naturally you will ignore these.

14 WAYS OF DISREGARDING SOCIAL ETIQUETTE AT A DINNER PARTY

1. Slurp your soup so loudly that it sounds like bath water disappearing down the plug hole.
2. Blow your nose on the linen napkin.
3. Clutch two bread rolls to your chest in an impression of Melinda Messenger.
4. Play an imaginary tune on a breadstick, pretending that you're Ian Anderson of Jethro Tull.

5. Insert a breadstick up each nostril.

6. Do crude drawings of naked women on your napkin.

7. Deliberately call your host's husband 'Don' instead of Ron and see how long it takes for him to correct you. When he finally puts you right, apologise profusely, but carry on calling him 'Don'. His face should turn a nice purple colour.

8. Beforehand, slip a short and curly into your pocket and produce it half way through your meal, claiming that you found the hair in your food. The host will be beside herself with grief, especially since it is clearly not from your head. A few minutes later, repeat the trick with a tiny stone. By now, the host – her reputation in tatters – will be on the line to the Samaritans. Round it off shortly afterwards by producing a used condom, insisting that you found that also in the goulash. The penny will finally drop and, if they don't see the funny side and ask you to leave, that's an added bonus.

9. Spend much of the evening adjusting your underwear, helpfully explaining that the trouble with these new pants is that they keep riding up the crack in your arse.

10. Scoff all the after-dinner mints.

11. Promise that you have perfected the art of pulling the tablecloth away without smashing any crockery or glassware. Afterwards, offer to pay for the breakages.

12. Start a dirty limerick competition.

13. Drop your trousers and blow out the candle with a mighty fart.

14. Suggest a game of charades, but get bored after *Free Willy* and *Leave It To Beever*.

If your behaviour doesn't guarantee that you'll never get invited again, your topics of conversation will. Here are a few subjects likely to break the ice as well as the host's heart:

- The merits of hanging, drawing and quartering as an alternative punishment to community service.

- Places your tongue has been.

- Places your dog's tongue has been.

- Big hairy spiders.

- Botulism.

- How women only get decent jobs by sleeping their way to the top.

- How a woman's place is in the home.

- Your intestines.

- Nicholas Witchell.

- Thrush.

- A baboon's arse.

- What you'd like to do to Liz Hurley.

- How millions are starving while you're tucking into this sumptuous repast.

SITUATIONS

- Dermatitis.

- Topless models.

- The crusty stuff that you find in your eyes first thing in the morning.

- Irritable bowel syndrome.

- How all women are gagging for it.

- Cradle cap.

- Michael Portillo.

- Declining the verb 'to masturbate', including pluperfect, conditional and imperfect tenses.

- Amputation.

- How boring dinner parties are.

Eat to the Beat

FOOD AND DRINK

Vegetarians. What do they get off on? They always look so serious, so intense, so dictatorial. If you ever have the misfortune to go to somebody's house and have a veggie meal plonked down in front of you, explain that it's against your religion to eat anything that didn't once have parents. Animals are meant to be eaten. It's the same with fish. If God had intended cod or haddock for another purpose in life, he'd have made them better-looking. The only thing more boring than a vegetarian is a group of vegetarians. You go out with them for a good pig-out and they eat a lettuce leaf and give you a lecture. They make you think you're sub-human, but, then again, they could discover that anyway if they stuck around for a few weeks. The one redeeming feature about veggie girls is they do stay nice and trim, but, with all that green stuff, their farts smell awful. And you've to ask yourself: if a girl doesn't like meat, how will she react to having a champion sausage inside her?

A spectacular way of ending a relationship with a veggie girl (and a much cheaper one than buying her a fur coat) is to cook her a soya pie and confess afterwards that the soya was really mince. The fall-out will make Chernobyl seem tame. A less subtle method of calling it a day is to arrive home from the office with a dead pig under your arm, but you may have to pay for two fares on the Underground. Or you could drop your pants and say, 'Want to get your mouth around my black pudding?' You won't see her for dust.

8 THINGS TO TRY WITH FOOD AND DRINK

1. Go on a binge of curry and dried fruit, a diet designed for maximum anal action.
2. Sprinkle some cayenne pepper in your granny's Horlicks.
3. If your flatmate's going out on a hot date, slip some extra garlic into the evening meal without telling him.
4. If he's a chilli freak, add a few senna pods to keep him on the go. But remember to make sure you eat something different or you'll both be pebble-dashing the bathroom walls.
5. Order a chicken madras takeaway to be sent to the home of a couple of vegans.
6. Phone up a dozen different pizza companies and order a pizza from each to be sent round to your mate's address.
7. If you're going to be sick, do it over a tramp. At least, that way he'll have a hot meal. And if some do-gooding old dear passes by and mutters, 'Poor wretch,' you can snap back: 'Well actually, I thought it was quite a good one.'

9 THINGS THAT SMELL WORSE THAN EGGS

1. A student's socks.

2. A wrestler's jock-strap.

3. Your boss's breath.

4. A giraffe's arse.

5. Your uncle's armpits if he hasn't used deodorant.

6. Your uncle's armpits if he's used Brut.

7. A baby's nappy.

8. A room full of steaming wet pacamacs.

9. A cabbage growers' convention.

Pulling Mussels from the Shell

THE GREAT HOLIDAY EXPERIENCE

It's that time of year again when you start planning your summer holiday. Anthea Turner is lying by the pool in a pleasantly skimpy swimsuit while Judith Chalmers's pink dress is scaring the life out of a couple of Dartmoor ponies and some bird you've never heard of with a permagrin is telling you what a wonderful city Paris is, glossing over the fact that it's inhabited by rather a lot of French people. It all makes you think of the three S's – sun, sea and sex. Forget about the surf – that's just for annoyingly handsome posers whose taut stomach muscles are still five years away from developing into a beer gut. Let's see whether Anthea wants to rub Ambre Solaire into them then!

Along with pubs and parties, a holiday can be the most edifying experience of your life. After all, it's got the two main ingredients for a good time – birds and booze, both of which come much cheaper on holiday than anywhere else. Single lads go on holiday in search of meaningless sex, often with girls whose name they can't pronounce and always with girls whose name they will have forgotten the next day. Since this is a prime requisite when choosing a destination, why don't travel brochures include amongst their myriad of symbols a furry triangle to indicate that this is a resort where only Norman Wisdom could fail to pull?

Choosing where to go on holiday is the toughest decision of all, particularly since brochures can make anywhere seem appealing. You know full well that the local photographer rushed out to take all his pictures of Rhyl on the one sunny day last year. And all the photos of idyllic, sun-kissed foreign beaches somehow fail to show the pack of rabid dogs fighting over the remains of your lunch or the ceremonial hoisting of the German national flag. So to stay in Britain or to go abroad is no easy choice. You have to weigh up the pros and cons.

11 REASONS FOR HOLIDAYING IN BRITAIN

1. The weather is never a disappointment because you know in advance that it's going to chuck it down for two weeks.
2. No dodgy foreign food or water to worry about. So you don't have to incur excess baggage charges over endless bottles of diarrhoea tablets.
3. No dodgy foreigners to worry about.
4. You don't have to spend weeks mugging up on the local currency or language. 'Gi'us a pint' is as widely recognized in Newquay as it is in Blackpool.
5. You're unlikely to get travel-sick, unless crossing the Devon border brings you out in a rash.
6. You won't spend the whole fortnight eating some close relative of Spam.
7. You get proper fish and chips.
8. You won't miss any episodes of *EastEnders*.
9. You don't have to wait till the next day to read all the football news in the paper.

10. Your postcards arrive home before you do.

11. You're never far from a model village.

12 REASONS FOR HOLIDAYING ABROAD

1. You can get pissed on the flight.

2. International totty. At the right resort, you can work your way through every UN member country in a fortnight, although you may wish to skip Moldova.

3. Your hotelier won't be some Nora Batty clone with a list of regulations which make the Maastricht Treaty look concise.

4. If you're out after 10pm, you don't risk being locked out for the night.

5. There's no danger of being invaded by the Radio 1 Roadshow.

6. People don't spend the entire summer grumbling about the weather.

7. The sea looks invitingly blue, instead of a sludgy brown colour peppered with dog turds, and warm, instead of a constant temperature barely above freezing point.

8. Jim Davidson won't be appearing in summer season (though it's best to check in advance, just in case).

9. There are no piers in danger of imminent collapse.

10. You get smart sun loungers instead of tatty deckchairs which take off the tip of your little finger while you are trying to put them up in a force-eight gale.

11. The opportunity to study a wide variety of insect life – often in your room.

12. You can buy chocolate bars with rude names.

On Holidaying in Britain

You've thought it all through and, after careful consideration, you and your mates have opted for a holiday in Britain, thus exposing yourself to a torrent of kiss-me-quick hats, candy floss, amusement arcades, homicidal seagulls, incontinent donkeys on the beach and that great British seaside tradition where all the OAPs huddle together in the shelters along the prom on a wet and windy Sunday morning to read the *News of the World*. All British resorts have more than their rightful allocation of wrinklies, many of whom return to the same place year after year to pay their respects to those lost in previous skirmishes when the dinner gong sounded to herald the stampede for the Brown Windsor soup.

Therefore the secret is to choose a place where the nightlife consists of more than bingo, whist drives and some bloke on his mighty organ. You might think a good way of ensuring this is to book into a four-star hotel which offers live entertainment. Wrong. The words to beware of in these instances are 'international' and 'cabaret'. An 'international artiste' will be some old boiler from Oldham in sequins and rouge who spends most of her life on Mediterranean cruises butchering other people's songs. She will say things like, 'This song has been very good to me' before spectacularly failing to return the compliment. 'Cabaret' is even worse. This means you'll be subjected to some Spanish juggler, one of those people who do strange things with hoops, or a fifth-rate magic act where the assistant is usually quite fit, but utterly brain-dead. And don't even be lured by the promise of the thrice-weekly hotel disco. It will just be a few sad old men turning back the clock with their wives to the sounds of "Stayin' Alive" and "Night Fever".

The alternative is a bed and breakfast. It has the advantage of being much cheaper and, in theory, offers you greater freedom. You will soon find, however, that a life sentence at Wormwood Scrubs will grant you more freedom than you'll get at a seaside guest house.

23 WAYS OF ANNOYING A BRITISH LANDLADY

1. Bring sand into the guest house on the soles of your trainers.
2. Bring a girl back to your room.
3. Talk in your room after 10.30pm.
4. Have more than one bath a week.
5. Turn up two minutes late for dinner.
6. Ask whether there is a porter to carry your cases.
7. Return to the guest house with a hint of alcohol on your breath.
8. Ask for a night key.
9. Creak the stairs on the way to your room at night.
10. Wear loud shirts.
11. Go into the dining room in shorts.
12. Complain about the fungus growing on your bed sheets.
13. Complain that the window in your room doesn't shut properly and therefore leaves a one-inch gap through which a howling wind blows every night.
14. Complain about getting only one sausage for breakfast.
15. Complain about the view from your room – the septic tank and sewage works.
16. Complain about anything.

17. Move any of the ornaments in your room without prior written permission.

18. Ask to see the menu.

19. Ask whether you could have breakfast a little later.

20. Ask for an alarm call.

21. Ring for room service.

22. Go down with a serious dose of flu so that you are unable to vacate your room at 9.30am sharp.

23. Look as if you are enjoying yourself.

Since so many things are guaranteed to incur her wrath, there's not much point in holding back. You and your mates might as well have some fun. Try the following:

- Sound the fire alarm in the dead of night so that all the residents have to wander out into the street in their pyjamas.

- Sound the dinner gong half an hour early so that all of the guests come down too soon and have to be sent back to their rooms.

- Long-standing residents will have their favourite chairs in the lounge. Get down early with your mates, occupy the best seats and wait for the look of horror on the guests' faces as they realize that they have been gazumped.

- Pull the aerial out of the socket at the back of the television set shortly before they all gather to watch *Coronation Street*.

- Pretend to go sleepwalking in the middle of the night and knock on the door of the landlady's bedroom. When she interrogates you in the morning, insist that you can't remember a thing, but admit that it has happened before.

- Slip a love note under the landlady's door, purportedly from the old boy in room 4.

- Booby trap the lounge door so that a bucket of water falls on the first person who opens it.

- Have a fire extinguisher fight on the landing.

- At dinner, offer to pull the chair out for one of the more matronly guests. While she is thanking you for being a perfect gentleman, slip a whoopee cushion on to the seat.

- Start a bread roll fight at dinner.

- Leave a set of false teeth on one of the tables, informing the landlady that a guest must have left them behind at dinner. Watch with glee as she tries to find out who they belong to.

- After dinner, make sure that you and your mates occupy the only available toilets for at least half an hour. A queue of old folk, increasingly desperate to relieve their bladders, will build up outside.

- Add a few squirts of washing-up liquid to the ornamental fountain in the front garden. Soon it will be overflowing with foam.

- Keep ringing the bell on reception and disappearing.

- Hang on a sign on the landlady's door, reading: Massage £10; Hand Relief £25; Blow Job £50.

- Go down to dinner stark naked.

Once she finds out that you're behind these various incidents, you'll almost certainly be thrown out, but that is the probably the best thing that could happen to your holiday. And you can now turn your attentions to leaving your mark on the rest of the resort. Turning signposts around and mooning at passers-by are all very well, but they're pretty juvenile, and you wouldn't want to be thought of like that, would you? So, why not collect the stray coke cans, empty beer bottles, paper bags, ice lolly sticks, the odd dead seagull and the occasional oil slick and build your own work of art on the beach in the form of a phallic sandcastle? Another particularly satisfying sight is watching a family set out a vast picnic on the beach and then have to snatch it up in a hurry as the tide rushes in. So if a group bearing hampers and rugs settle down near the water's edge, assure them that the tide is on the way out when, in fact, you know different. Then retreat to the safety of the promenade as it suddenly dawns on them that their egg and cress sandwiches are about to float out to sea.

The other thing to remember about British seaside resorts is that they're essentially quiet. They only come alive between 9pm and 2am (June to August) before returning to a state of slumber. So a sure way of upsetting the locals is to make a noise outside of these hours. A rowdy conga down the High Street at three in the morning is guaranteed to bring a friendly visit from the constabulary and a flood of angry correspondence to the letters page in the local paper.

Still, you mustn't lose sight of what you're really on holiday for – sex. These briefs encounters are loosely known as 'holiday romances', but let's be honest romance never enters the equation. It's just hello, bonk, goodbye. So you don't want to waste your time on a girl who wants something more permanent. You want to cut out the long-winded chat-up ritual of favourite band, favourite colour, favourite vegetable and go straight to favourite position. As an opening gambit, look wistfully into her eyes and muse: 'I wonder what it's like under the pier at midnight.' If she answers 'crowded', you're in. The general rule with these engagements is that if you haven't received a firm commitment after buying her one bacardi and coke, move on to somebody else. However, some girls are best given a wide berth, no matter how willing they may appear. Avoid any girl with 'Hell's Angels Windsor Chapter' on the back of her jacket.

On Holidaying Abroad

So you've gone for the foreign option, no doubt encouraged by all those tales of Club 18–30 holidays and stories about girls behaving badly in Ibiza. In some respects, going on holiday abroad is like shopping at Sainsbury's, whereas holidaying in Britain is like your corner shop. The trouble is that while there are many more tasty items on offer in Sainsbury's (in the form of Scandinavian, Italian and French chicks), there is also fiercer competition. Better-looking shoppers in the shape of bronzed Italian and Spanish lads often swipe the best stuff off the shelf before the pasty-skinned Brits get a look in. And when we try to compete, we end up with a severe case of sunburn, making any form of sexual activity a painful experience. Not many positions in *The Joy of Sex* cater for red-raw shoulders and thighs on which you could char-grill a steak.

Your first experience on arriving in a foreign land will be the customs officers at the airport. They may all look like members of a Mexican firing squad, but they are only trying to do their job. So it is best not to antagonize them with any smart-alec remarks. When they ask whether you have anything to declare, don't reply, 'Only the crack in my arse,' because the next thing you know you'll be strip-searched and have a couple of Labradors sniffing your backside.

Assuming you make it through customs, your next point of contact will be your travel company rep. The popular assumption is that travel reps are desperate for a reminder of Britain and will therefore jump in the sack with anyone sporting a pair of Union Jack boxer shorts. The chances are, though, that they took a job abroad just to get away from British men and are already spoken for by some hulking Latin Romeo who runs one of the local bars. Besides, they're probably the subject of some fly-on-the-wall docu-soap and you don't really want your infidelities to get back to your girlfriend in England via a six-part series on BBC 1.

The great thing about foreign beaches is that girls go topless at the drop of a hat – or, to be more accurate, the drop of a bra. This is something you just don't get in Morecambe in September unless they're acclimatizing themselves for a forthcoming polar expedition. It is important to strike up a conversation with these busty beauties as quickly as possible and what more natural way than if your beach ball should accidentally happen to stray in their direction? One of the following lines might set the ball rolling, as it were:

- 'Can I have my ball back please?'

- 'I like all-over tans.'

- 'Nice tits!'

The first thing to ascertain is where she's from. You don't want to start slagging off the number of Germans on the beach, only to discover she's from Hamburg, or ridicule the Italians' status as a warrior nation and then learn that she's from Milan. Once you've established that, it's probably a shrewd move to find out what she thinks of the English before admitting where you're from. If she spits on the sand and snorts 'feelthy pigs' at the mere mention of England, it is best either to put on a phoney Italian accent or seek out another girl. On the other hand, if she thinks English boys are cute, it not only means that you're in with a chance, but also that she probably thinks Great White Sharks are cute too.

The way to a foreign bird's heart is via her tongue. Mutter a few words in her language and she'll be yours for at least the next half-hour. It might be the only bit of GCSE German or French you can remember (for Italian and Spanish, just add an 'o') and whereas 'where is my aunt's pen?' is not recognized as a great chat-up line in Bridlington, *'ou est la plume de ma tante?'* will do the business with a little lovely from Bordeaux. It doesn't matter how much gibberish you talk or however Clouseau-like your accent is – she will delight in gently correcting you. Your ineptitude will be your tool. Better that than the other way round. Her French resistance will crumble and, before you know it, you'll be playing trains and tunnels.

A holiday abroad also enables you to wind up the various other nationalities at your resort – preferably without starting World War Three.

On the Beach

- Yell 'Shark!' when the sea is full of bathers.

- Confiscate any frisbee which heads in your direction.

- As you run to the water's edge, kick sand at sunbathers on the way. This is a popular sport with all European holidaymakers.

- Erect your sun lounge and umbrella right in the middle of the Germans' game of volleyball.

- Drip ice cream on to the bodies of sunbathers as you pass.

- Have a water-bag fight, soaking everyone within range.

At the Pool

- Creep down at the crack of dawn and remove all the Germans' towels from the sun loungers. Replace them with your own.

- Dive underwater and resurface so that your head comes up between a girl's legs. Protest your innocence.

- Dive underwater and emerge with your swimming trunks on your head. In some resorts, this will clear the pool faster than a turd alert.

- If there's a spare bed in your hotel room, use the mattress as a li-lo.

- Order a round of drinks from the poolside bar and put them on somebody else's room number.

- Volunteer your services for the game of water polo so that you can grope all the women in an apparently legitimate quest for the ball.

- Volunteer for the aerobics class and stand at the back so that you get a good view when the girls bend over.

- Volunteer for any activity which is mixed.

In your Hotel

- Never make your bed in the morning, but leave a pair of sweaty pants on the top so that the maid has to move them before going about her chores.

- Slip a rubber snake in your bed near the pillow and fold over the sheets roughly. When the maid pulls them back to make the bed properly, she'll get the shock of her life.

- Leave soaking wet towels and piles of sand on the bathroom floor.

- Hang T-shirts with rude slogans over your balcony.

- If you suspect the maid is helping herself to your drinks, spit in an empty bottle of Lucozade, mark the level on the bottle and see if she takes the bait. If she doesn't try it again, wait until she complains to the management or is rushed to hospital, and then you'll know she did.

Silence is Golden

AT THE LIBRARY

Although libraries are designed to serve as seats of learning, anybody who has ever tried to study in one will tell you that they also double up as a haven for anyone with four bags of shopping needing a sit-down and a gossip, anyone with a permanent hacking cough and anyone at all within a five-mile radius when it's raining. Libraries also seem to attract simple folk who express amazement at having to pay a fine for returning a book three years late, plus legions of old dears in search of their family trees who celebrate each find with a shriek of delight worthy of scoring the winning goal in a Cup final. Entire classes of supposedly disruptive school children can pass in and out of a library without so much as a murmur, but if an old biddy discovers that Great Uncle Cedric was a direct descendant of Wat Tyler, the whole town has to know about it. The rule that you must be silent in a library only applies to those unable to produce a bus pass.

In the face of such stiff competition, it is therefore a tall order to be more annoying than the regular inhabitants of a library, but here are a few suggestions which may help:

- Hide behind the supernatural section and go 'Boo!' whenever anyone removes a book from the shelf.

- Lurk behind the sex help section and make heavy breathing noises.

- Snigger and point at anybody browsing at books on sexually transmitted diseases.

- Read out loud.

- Start a sing-song.

- Burst a succession of paper bags.

- Whistle every Beatles song you can think of.

- Drum your fingers on the table for half an hour.

- If the person opposite you is reading a newspaper and insists on folding it and unfolding it as noisily as possible, set fire to the bottom of the page.

- Complain that you can't find the section on map reading.

- See how many books you can balance in a pile on the table before they all come crashing down.

- Ask the librarian to keep the noise down when she is serving a customer.

- Ask the librarian where the menswear section is. When she looks puzzled and explains that this is a library, say 'Oh, sorry' and leave.

- With a suggestive leer, ask the librarian whether she knows where you might find a Trollope.

- Ask the librarian in a loud voice whether she has got anything that will improve your sex life.

- At the subject index, call across to the librarian and ask whether 'bestiality' comes before 'buggery'.

- Then ask her whether 'foreplay' comes before 'fucking'. If she says, 'Not in my house,' you could be in.

I Love My Dog

OWNING A PET

No wonder a dog is supposed to be man's best friend. We have so much in common: we both put on the big, doe-eyed look when we've done something wrong; both of us roll over on our back and wave our legs in the air at the first sign of affection; both are eminently capable of behaving badly in public; and both will do anything for a chocolate button. Sadly the similarities end when it comes to the ability to lick one's own arse.

Owning a dog is a big responsibility, but it can also bring you years of pleasure.

18 WAYS TO BEHAVE BADLY AS A DOG OWNER

1. Encourage your mongrel to mate with all the local pedigree bitches.
2. Tell your dog that cousin Eric is a stick.
3. Laugh like a drain when your dog mates with your aunt's leg.
4. Allow your dog to join in a Sunday morning football match.
5. Allow your dog to run on to a bowling green in the middle of a match.
6. Encourage your dog to bark in the middle of the night.
7. Allow your dog to run over other people's property, digging up as many plants as possible.

8. Encourage your dog to try and lick your mother-in-law in a rude place.

9. If your dad comes to visit, throw one of his slippers to the dog to play with.

10. Teach your dog to growl at trick-or-treaters, carol singers or any other pesky kids who come knocking on your door.

11. Teach your dog to snarl at any caller who uses the words 'double glazing'.

12. When you've got friends around, get your dog to retrieve your girlfriend's knickers from the bedroom.

13. Get your dog to hide behind the hedge whenever the postman calls and then to leap out at him as he walks up the path.

14. If you've got a big dog, encourage it to scare the hell out of toy poodles.

15. Encourage your dog to chase cyclists or anyone on a zimmer frame.

16. After your dog has been for a swim, make sure it shakes itself dry over somebody's picnic.

17. Watch your dog race up to a stranger in pale clothes, jump up at them and put muddy paw prints all over them. After ten seconds or so, order your dog to get down. This is another secret dog-owner's rule.

I'm in the Mood for Dancing

PARTY PARTY

A good party can make your week, but unless you're Mr. Popular sometimes it seems that the only way you can get an invite is to throw your own. However that's too much like hard work and anyway trashing your own home is something of a self-defeating exercise. So a better move is to ingratiate yourself with the host – compliments, flowers, proposal of marriage – anything to secure an invitation. Naturally, this works better if the host is female. If the host is male, the promise that you'll bring crates full of lager and won't try to cop off with the bird he fancies should do the trick.

Alas, occasionally even the best-laid plans come to grief and you find that the host won't take the hint. On these occasions, it may be necessary to resort to more drastic methods.

15 LINES TO USE TO GATECRASH YOUR WAY INTO A PARTY

1. 'Flying Squad! This is a raid.'
2. 'I'm a friend of Julie's.'
3. 'I'm a friend of Big Alf, the local enforcer.'
4. 'I'm a friend of Leonardo DiCaprio's. Leo's waiting outside to see if I can wangle him an invite.'
5. 'I am an alien. Take me to your leader.'
6. 'I'm the strippagram.'
7. 'Darling. Remember me? We met on holiday eight years ago. Of course you do...'
8. 'I'm from the local council and I'm here to conduct a survey of what young people get up to on a Saturday night. I'll start in the lounge.'
9. 'I'm from Ritzy's nightclub and I'm here to hand out free vouchers for February.'
10. 'I'm here to read the meter.'
11. 'I bring gifts of gold, frankincense and Malibu.'
12. 'I've parked my Ferrari round the corner. Is that OK?'
13. 'I'm from Camelot.'
14. 'I absolutely adore washing up.'
15. 'Please can I come in? It's raining.'

5 LINES NOT TO USE TO GATECRASH YOUR WAY INTO A PARTY

1. 'I'm a Jehovah's Witness.'
2. 'Can I interest you in double glazing?'
3. 'Would you like to buy some dusters?'
4. 'I'm from the Temperance Society.'
5. 'I'm the life and soul of any party, but particularly the Conservatives. As you probably know, there are local elections next Thursday and I was wondering whether I could count on...'

Once inside, you need to establish your territory for the evening, rather like a tom cat, although spraying the furniture is optional. Ideally, you want to position yourself at the centre of the action. With most parties, this means the toilet, but, as you know only too well from past experience, spending five hours in the bog is not the most tantalizing prospect. Those who are about as much of a party animal as Howard Hughes will gravitate towards the kitchen where two dullards will stand on sentry duty at the doorway like the Sheriff of Nottingham's men in *Robin Hood*. If you're going to spend an entire party in the kitchen, you might as well stand outside in the street, because you're missing out on all the action, unless you happen to be at one of those rare gatherings where couples have steamy sex across the oven hob. The advantages of lurking in the kitchen are that you have easy access to the nibbles and booze and there is a constant flow of visitors, but even you will tire of hearing yourself say, 'Those cheese dips are nice' for the 52nd time. Besides, every bird knows that the only men who stay in the kitchen at parties are either Gary Rhodes or the socially inept. You might as well have 'Saddo' scrawled in ink on your forehead.

No, the only place to be is the lounge where the music is pounding and bodies are swaying. The party is unique in a man's life insofar as pulling actually takes second place to drinking. With so much free booze on offer, a party is a true Santa's grotto and it is almost sacrilege to have your hands parted from a can for more than 30 seconds. However you don't want to go home without a present so it's a question of when is the best time to get out your Tonka toy. Some schools of thought favour bedding the first girl you set eyes on within ten minutes of walking through the door; others recommend a more patient approach. There are points for and against going in for the quick kill.

For

- If you stumble across a bird who's a dead ringer for Louise, you don't want to risk losing her to some flash git.

- Having got your name on the scoresheet, it leaves you free to concentrate on drinking yourself stupid for the rest of the evening.

- By getting your end away early on in proceedings, there is at least some chance of a satisfactory performance between the sheets. By the end of the evening, you'll be a slobbering wreck whose duvet dialogue will be limited to 'Sorry'.

- There will be stiff competition for bed space as the party winds down and you could end up trying your luck in the potting shed.

Against

- By going to bed early, you risk having all the coats thrown over you.

- You may miss out on the chicken vol-au-vents.

- You may blow all the love juices you can muster on some old dog when there's a pedigree bitch gagging for it.

- By leaving your charge until everyone is as mellow as a newt, your chosen partner probably won't remember anything about it the following morning. This is always a good idea if you were embarrassingly poor or if she happens to be married to the local psycho.

The biggest barrier to your chances of success on the totty front is being stuck with the party bore. Whilst the majority of guests with a charisma by-pass will have had the sense to remain in the kitchen, there is always one who thinks he can graduate to the lounge. He is easily recognisable by his Hawaiian shirt and large red glasses – both worn to try and give him a personality – but because he knows no fear he is a dangerous adversary. He will latch on to anybody appearing, albeit momentarily, to be at a loose end and subject them to a stream of amusing anecdotes from the wacky world of sanitation inspectors. Worse still, since he probably hasn't got a friend in the world, he will suggest that you hunt in pairs to pull the best-looking birds. This is akin to going to the hottest nightclub in town with Quasimodo in tow. Apart from anything else, all the available talent will think that this dipstick you have never met in your life before is a mate of yours and will therefore immediately abandon any plans they may have had to get acquainted with the contents of your underpants. You could of course tell him that you've been wanting to shake him off for ages, but this might give him the wrong idea. Instead one of the following phrases may prove more effective in getting rid of your unwelcome sidekick:

• 'Excuse me, but I'm just off to talk to someone interesting.'

• 'I think I'm losing the will to live.'

• 'And I thought the new gun laws had got rid of small bores.'

• 'Ah, here's my friend Terry. He breeds maggots.'

If the party is any good, at some stage you will almost certainly feel the need to throw up. Given that there is already a long queue for the loo, you will have to find an alternative receptacle. But be as discreet as possible – the sight of you honking and heaving may just deter potential bedmates.

8 DISCREET PLACES TO BE SICK AT A PARTY

1. Behind a curtain.
2. Over the cheese and tomato flan in the fridge.
3. In a pot-plant holder.
4. In the budgie's cage.
5. Under a cushion on the sofa (unless there's someone sitting on it at the time).
6. Under the bed.

7. On a yellow and brown carpet, flecked with red.

8. Over the party bore.

8 INDISCREET PLACES TO BE SICK AT A PARTY

1. Down a curtain.

2. Over the CD player.

3. In the rottweiller's bowl.

4. Over the host.

5. Over a copulating couple.

6. Down the dress of the girl you are about to ask to dance.

7. Over the naked body of the girl you are about to shag.

8. Over yourself.

Don't worry if you disgrace yourself at someone else's party – you'll be in good company. Indeed, you're more likely to be remembered for all the wrong reasons if you stayed stone-cold sober and spent the entire evening sitting in the corner thumbing through back copies of *Reader's Digest*. Still, there are some actions guaranteed to ensure that you won't be invited again.

9 WAYS OF BEHAVING BADLY AT A PARTY

1. Instead of bringing a bottle or cans of lager, bring your holiday slides.

2. Cop off with the host's wife.

3. Get caught rodgering the family nanny.

4. Be found face down in the bowl of taramosalata.

5. Call the police just after midnight to complain of a disturbance.

6. Keep drinking out of everyone else's glass or can.

7. Pile your plate a foot high with all the best food before anyone else gets a look-in.

8. Get caught in bed in a drunken stupor whispering sweet nothings in the ear of the family Afghan hound.

9. Leave with the family jewels.

Arranging Your Own Party

If none of your friends want to risk their home by staging a party, you'll have to show them how it's done. It won't be the first time you've held your own, but it will be the first time you have with 50 people present. The guest list is always a tricky one. The obvious temptation is to invite all your ugliest mates so that the best-looking babes are fighting each other to get to you. However, the reality is that they'll take one look at what's on offer and bugger off five minutes after arriving. Therefore a more sensible course of action is to invite a good cross-section of blokes and girls and make sure you're the number one choice by systematically wrecking your mates' chances (*see page 58*). As the host, you do have an instant advantage anyway. If it's a good party, the girls will be grateful to you for inviting them. Whether that gratitude extends to sucking your todger remains to be seen.

8 PEOPLE NOT TO INVITE TO YOUR PARTY

1. Your parents.
2. Your granny.
3. Your local vicar.

4. A delegation of Russian fishermen.

5. The South-East London Meths Drinkers' Society.

6. Boyzone.

7. Hannibal Lecter.

8. Members of the local noise abatement society.

You may decide to go for a theme party with everyone coming in fancy dress, but remember that some costumes are more conducive to trouble-free sex than others. If you have to spend as much time fumbling around her zip to find the way in as you do trying to get your front door key into the keyhole in the early hours of the morning, don't be surprised if she goes off the idea and asks you to call her a cab home. For this, and other reasons, the following themes should be avoided:

- A deep-sea diving party – everyone in wet suits, flippers and snorkels plus oxygen cylinders on their backs.

- A mountaineering party – everyone in heavy boots, more oxygen equipment and carrying a tent.

- A medieval knights party – everyone in suits of armour and chain mail, brandishing heavy swords.

- A tinned peach party – everybody's already stoned when they arrive.

- An impotence party – nobody will come.

Saved by the Bell

AT SCHOOL AND COLLEGE

According to the brochures, school and college days are supposed to be the best of your life, which means it is essential that they aren't for your teachers or tutors. Being at college is a war of attrition. Whilst you are there to learn a few things, the inescapable fact is that the ability to put one over on another adult will stand you in greater stead in life than knowing that the battle of Marston Moor was fought in 1644. And the beauty of it is that the tutors are aware of the rules too. They know that despite the fact that you're now classed as young adults, you're still fourth formers at heart and are hell-bent on revenge for the months of slavery imposed by GCSEs. So they enter every classroom half expecting to be greeted by flour bombs or to find that their chair has been booby trapped. Obviously there are limits to these pranks. If you find yourself attending your tutor's funeral five days later, it probably means you've gone too far.

7 WAYS OF IRRITATING YOUR TUTOR

1. Lock him out of the classroom.

2. Get the whole class to go to the wrong room.

3. During a difficult test, ask whether you can pop to the loo. Instead set off the fire alarm so that the test has to be abandoned.

4. Modern desks are little more than tables, held together by screws. Remove all the leg screws beforehand so that the desktop is just resting on them. The moment your tutor puts down a heavy book or his briefcase on the surface, the whole lot should collapse.

5. If there's a payphone in the corridor, smear the earpiece with ink and, as your tutor passes, tell him there's a call for him.

6. Get a mate to ring the college during a lecture with an urgent message for your tutor. By the time he gets to the staff room, realizes that nobody's there (because your mate has hung up) and returns to the classroom, it should have wasted a good ten minutes.

7. Speak only in rhyme throughout the lesson and encourage your fellow students to follow suit.

I Wish it Could Be Christmas Every Day

FESTIVE FROLICS

If we need to look at just one way in which the world has improved over the last 1999 years, we only have to think of Christmas. Whereas back then, there was no room at the inn for Mary and Joseph and so the baby Jesus had to be born in a stable, now there's room in the inn for everyone and with all day opening and an extension till midnight, there's no excuse for anybody not getting into the festive spirit. Christmas may be a time for giving and receiving, but above all it's a time for getting ratted in one long, alcoholic haze stretching from the first office party right through to New Year's Day with time off only for Rolf Harris's *Christmas Animal Hospital*. Purists moan that the true meaning of Christmas has been lost in recent years, but whenever we open another grossly hideous pair of socks from Great Aunt Hermione in Bognor Regis, our immediate reaction is 'Jesus Christ!'

Buying a suitable present can be the toughest part of Christmas. People have this strange urge to buy animals, but remember, a puppy isn't just for Christmas. Since all your family claim to take so long choosing the ideal gift, but always manage to come up with something dreadful, you might as well save yourself a lot of time and effort and settle for purchasing presents that are deliberately inappropriate. So how about a skateboard for your granny? What about a nose stud for Uncle Cyril, doyen of the cardigan? And for your horrible little nephew, how about a game of roulette... the Russian version?

There are basically two distinct types of Christmas – a family Christmas and an enjoyable one. For a family gathering, you team up with the deaf and the incontinent spanning the three generations or more of your family. Relatives you haven't seen for eons – and with good reason – tell you how much you've grown, politely suggest that you get your hair cut and give you 50p as an extra Christmas treat with which to buy some new clothes. At the other end of the age scale, nephews and nieces gorge such vast quantities of turkey, ice cream and Coca-Cola that they are a constant threat to anyone passing within vomiting range. Auntie Ivy is delighted to see that you are wearing the pink frilly shirt she bought you, but little does she know that just by taking it out of its box you are being ironic and that it is only being worn in the hope that one of the attendant brats will throw up all over it.

The trouble with wearing one person's Christmas gift straight away is that you immediately alienate everyone else who has bought you clothing. Your mum, who has bought you an equally repulsive shirt, demands to know why you're not wearing her present. She can later be heard sobbing in the kitchen, basting the turkey with her tears and bits of loosened nasal fluid. The only way to keep everybody happy is to change shirts continually. With a confused and tipsy aunt in charge of the drinks cabinet, this has the added advantage that she'll keep thinking you're someone new who's arrived and will straight away offer you a drink. By changing shirts every half hour, you can be well away by the time the first cracker is pulled.

All through lunch they'll be saying, 'Mustn't miss the Queen's speech.' When the glorious hour arrives, however, they've all had so much sweet sherry and sparkling wine that they sleep right through it. Apart from the kids, you're the only one who's awake – and you couldn't give a toss. By the same token, you invariably get roped in to help with the dishes because you're the only one who can be relied upon not to convert the 32-piece dinner set into a 64-piece. Still, there's always a succession of parlour games to look forward to – in the same way that you would look forward to being crushed by a juggernaut.

But if you spend Christmas with your mates – or even by yourself – you don't have to worry whether or not 'London' is permissible because it's a proper name or whether 'tomato' is fruit or vegetable. You just get bladdered, listen to loud music and watch Swedish health videos instead of *Christmas Night with the Stars*. The only conceivable drawback is that you'll have to do your own cooking, but spaghetti hoops are a vastly underrated Christmas dish. Alternatively, there's bound to be some dodgy takeaway open.

Should you be unable to avoid the yuletide horror that is a family Christmas, here are a few tips to make the occasion more bearable.

- Tell the little brats that there are some presents hidden in the cellar and then lock the cellar door behind them. No one will hear their screams above the festive jollification and with any luck it will be Boxing Day before anybody realizes they are missing.

- Use only rude words in the compulsory game of Boggle.

- Tell any four-year-olds the truth about Father Christmas – that he's just a sad old man with an unhealthy interest in young children.

- Give everyone a neatly wrapped box of paper clips which you've nicked from the office and watch them struggle to find something complimentary to say about the gift. Someone is bound to come up with, 'Paper clips are always useful,' or, 'We're always running out.' Anybody who says 'What a crap present' is obviously worth getting to know.

- Buy your least favourite relative a novelty toy – or indeed anything – which explodes in their face.

- When pulling a Christmas cracker, loosen your grip at the last minute so that granny goes tumbling backwards off her chair and ends up in an undignified heap on the carpet.

- Insist that your painfully shy cousin does her impression of Cher. After a few bars, interrupt her and say, 'I really think this is too embarrassing to continue.'

- Get so pissed over lunch that you slump face first in the bowl of cranberry sauce.

- When the Christmas pudding is lit, turn a fire extinguisher on it.

- Sing the Sex Pistols' version of 'God Save the Queen' at the end of her speech.

- Use only porn film titles for the game of Charades. Watching your mum trying to mime *Take Me From Behind* or *Gerta and Brigitte Get Randy* will be worth the admission money alone.

- Write 'Plonker' on Uncle Peter's paper hat.

- Agree to be the hunter in Hide and Seek. Then when everyone has hidden, piss off down to the pub. Aunt Edna will still be hiding in the airing cupboard on New Year's Eve.

Driving in My Car

AT THE WHEEL

A man's car is very much an extension of his home. You can find the same boiled sweets, bits of chewing gum, empty cigarette packets and pen tops down the back seat of your car as you would down the back of your sofa. With any luck, this list of similarities will also extend to bras and knickers as your car-ignorant girlfriend finally manages to get her head around the big end. Still first you've actually got to persuade her to get into the back seat.

10 GOOD RESONS FOIR TELLING YOUR GIRLFRIENDTO CLIMB INTO THE BACK SEAT OF YOUR CAR

1. There's a much better view of a nearby electricity pylon from the back.
2. She'll be nearer the stereo speakers.
3. She'll be able to get a closer look at your nodding dog (this could be another euphemism).
4. The front door can be tricky to open.
5. If another vehicle smashes into the front of your stationary car, she'll be safer in the back.
6. If the engine should suddenly blow up, she'll be safer in the back.

7. If a falling meteorite should crash through your windscreen, she'll be less likely to be hit by flying glass in the back.

8. You want her to help you search for a lost £5 note.

9. You want her to help you search for El Dorado.

10. You want her to help you search for a missing mint.

You could also try to relieve her of items of clothing by playing on her ignorance about things mechanical. Begin by making the perfectly reasonable request that she takes off her tights in order that they be used to repair the broken fan belt. Then announce that your indicators have packed up and that you will need to wave something out of the driver's window to warn other motorists of your intentions. Her knickers would be just the job, leaving no road user in any doubt as to your intentions. Lastly, fret about your damaged front bumper and suggest that her bra, strategically placed, would help to cushion any impact. However, you should not be too optimistic about the success of any of these tactics.

Like your home, you should decorate your car to reflect your personality. How about a nice goat's head painted on the side or an enormous pair of breasts? However you should bear in mind that these designs may make your car more difficult to sell, especially if your would-be buyer is a little old lady. A less permanent fixture is a sticker for the rear windscreen. The slogan doesn't have to be as dull as 'Don't follow me – follow United' or 'I've seen the lions of Longleat', but it is best not to be too provocative in your choice of words. Thus car stickers to avoid putting up include:

- 'I'm pissed as a fart.'

- 'No tax, no insurance, no licence – who cares?'

- 'Death to cyclists.'

- 'All coppers are bastards.'

- 'Speed limits are for wimps.'

- 'Don't drink and drive – you spill too much.'

- 'If you can read this, you can probably see my bird giving me a blow job.'

The most frustrating period for any driver is being stuck in a traffic jam. You've got no choice but to sit there as time flashes by before you. It is worth bearing in mind that in the half hour you've been rendered motionless by a contraflow system which seems to link the M11 and Route 66, a total of 108 babies will have born in England, two Premiership managers will have been sacked and Michael Barrymore won't have said one funny thing on *Strike It Rich*. You're left with this feeling of helplessness, but what can you do to relieve the monotony?

- Wind down your window and start chatting up the nearest lady driver – unless she's got a 16-stone gorilla in the passenger seat.

- Sound your horn repeatedly to the tune of "La Cucaracha".

- If you're alone in the vehicle, see if you can pummel your personal gearstick to "Satisfaction" between car movements. No cheating, and even if you only go forward half a yard, you have to start all over again from Mr. Floppy. *Beware:* you may get some funny looks from other drivers.

- When you do go forward a few yards, make V signs at all the drivers you pass.

- With the windows down, conduct an imaginary argument between Hitler and Sir Jimmy Savile.

When you do finally hit the open road, you're bursting with ideas for day trips. And if you've got kids, there are so many exciting places to take them – places they would never have thought of asking to go:

9 HEARTLESS PLACES TO TAKE YOUR KIDS FOR THE DAY

1. Ramsgate in January when all the amusements are closed.
2. Ramsgate in summer.
3. A vet's surgery to see all the sick pets being put down.
4. On a ten-hour pub crawl.
5. To the finals of the World Bowls Championships.
6. To the dentist's, just for fun.
7. To school, even though it's closed for the holidays.
8. On a tour of the roundabouts of Basingstoke.
9. Somewhere they can eat lashings of pizza, jelly and ice cream, followed by a long, bumpy car ride home with no stops.

Chapter Three:

People

God Only Knows

JEHOVAH'S WITNESSES

For most of us, Jehovah's Witnesses are about as welcome in the house as dry rot or a Foster and Allen CD. They always appear so sinister, stalking purposefully along the road in pairs and dressed in black from head to toe like lost souls from a funeral cortège or ex-members of Iron Maiden. Some areas operate a Jehovah's Watch scheme whereby as soon as they are spotted in the neighbourhood, a network of phone calls from home to home makes sure that front doors are never opened. As a result, it must be a pretty thankless task as they end up with fewer conversions than the Japanese rugby team.

It wouldn't be so bad if you could have a good slanging match with them. When you get some pushy bloke canvassing on behalf of a new pizza parlour and you tell him you're too busy, you sometimes get a mouthful of abuse or, at best, a few dark mutterings. But no matter how rude you are to Jehovah's Witnesses, they are unfailingly polite. Either they will just shuffle away dejectedly or they will thank you for your time when you haven't even given them any. Perhaps they are being deeply ironic, but somehow you get the feeling that anyone who can traipse from door to door for hours on end peddling a product that nobody wants isn't blessed with a particularly well-developed sense of irony.

In view of their thick skins, it is not easy to shock a Jehovah's Witness. However it can be done.

20 WAYS TO BEHAVE BADLY IN FRONT OF JEHOVAH'S WITNESSES

1. Answer the door dressed as the Devil.
2. Set the dogs on them.
3. Set your girlfriend's mother on them.
4. Argue against the existence of the Lord for six hours, refusing to let them go.
5. Wire up the doorbell so that 10,000 volts go through them when they press it.
6. Say: 'Sorry, can't stop – I'm just shagging me bird.'
7. Say: 'Sorry, can't stop – I'm half-way through watching *Swedish Nymphets On Heat.*'
8. Say to the woman: 'Haven't I seen you hanging around King's Cross at night?'
9. Tell them that Bill Clinton is your God.
10. When they ask whether you've seen the light, tell them it's at the top of the stairs.
11. Scratch your bollocks throughout, bringing your hand up occasionally for inspection...
12. Then offer to shake them by the hand.
13. Leave your zip open and insert a raw sausage so that a little is protruding.
14. When they mention the Second Coming, wink at the bloke and say: 'So you're a twice-a-night guy then?'
15. Go to the door with an axe in your hand and with fake blood dripping from your mouth.
16. Offer them a slice of black pudding.
17. Say: 'What are your lot's views on self-abuse?'

18. Steer the conversation on to a discussion about the virtues of Melinda Messenger's tits.

19. Make repeated innuendoes about how the two of them celebrate a conversion.

20. Invite them in and sit them down next to the pile of copies of *Knave*.

Keep on Running

JOGGERS

You're out for a quiet walk in the park with your girlfriend. She's listening to the birds singing in the trees and you're listening to Test Match Special on Radio 4. She's despairing at England's disappearing woodland and you're despairing at England's inability to bat. 'What has become of the willow?' she sighs. 'It's just got an edge to third slip,' you groan.

Suddenly you hear puffing, panting and pounding of hooves behind you. Have you been enjoying the walk so much that you've accidentally strayed 250 miles on to the Grand National course? You turn round to see some wheezing prat, his face as red as his vest, bearing down on you. And is he going to run around you like any civilized human being? No way, because he's a jogger.

If the word 'jogger' were to come up on *Countdown* and Carol Vorderman were to get her consonants in a twist and give the answer as 'tosser', the contestants would be perfectly within their rights to say that the two words are one and the same. Jogging is supposed to be good for you, but have you ever seen a healthy looking jogger? They always look a split second away from a coronary. The only physical exercise blokes need is in the right arm, either for lifting a pint or for punishing Percy in the palm, or in the pelvic area for the few thrusts needed to keep a woman happy. Of course, women need to keep fit because, unlike men, they are prone to go to fat, and, let's face it, once they lose their shape they've got nothing left to offer. Still, there are healthier ways of doing it than jogging – washing your clothes, doing your ironing, tidying up after you, for example. Joggers represent a greater threat to the planet than global warming. Not only do they emit noxious gases, principally from their armpits and crotch, but they operate in the belief that they are above the law. Just as huntsmen will ride roughshod over anyone or anything to get at the fox, so joggers will plough through family photographs, picnics, knock over old ladies – whatever is needed to get from A to B without ever having to break stride.

This, if you'll pardon the expression, is their Achilles' heel. Force a jogger to break stride and you will make him exceedingly angry. So here are a few helpful suggestions:

13 WAYS TO FORCE A JOGGER TO BREAK STRIDE

1. When a jogger is approaching, start meandering wildly so that he doesn't know which way to go in order to avoid you.
2. Instead of holding a gate open for an approaching jogger, let it go at the last minute so that, after putting a spurt on to get there in time, he has to stop and open it.
3. Trip the bastard up as he goes past.
4. Set your dog on him.
5. Phone the police on your mobile and tell them that the bloke in the red and white track suit jogging around the lake answers the description of the armed robber on *Crimewatch* the other night.

6. Dig a large deep hole in his route and cover it with leaves. Hide behind a tree and wet yourself laughing as he disappears down the hole.

7. Tell an athletic-looking bloke that the jogger up ahead just stole a little lady's purse. Make yourself scarce by the time he has apprehended him and made a citizen's arrest.

8. Erect a trip-wire across his path.

9. Hide up a tree and drop an inflatable gorilla on his head as he passes beneath.

10. Hide up a tree and drop a bookcase on his head as he passes beneath. However, be careful with this – make sure you use an old bookcase that you don't mind ruining.

11. Insist on conducting a survey with the jogger about running shoes.

12. As he passes, tell him the back of his leg is bleeding profusely. Then see how fast you can run when he comes after you.

13. Line his route with land mines.

Message in a Bottle

THE MILKMAN

Unlike joggers, milkmen are thoroughly inoffensive creatures. They get up at some unearthly hour and drive a silly vehicle with the acceleration of a lawn mower, but always deliver your milk with a cheery smile. However, just because they appear to be decent blokes doesn't mean they're not fair game. And, as shift-workers know only too well, when you're not around, the milkman will jump into bed with your missus before you can say, 'An extra pint on Thursday, please.' It must be all that yoghurt which gives them the energy.

So just about the worst thing you can do to a milkman is arrive home early from work. The trail of gold tops leading from your bedroom window will be a bit of a giveaway, as, in the old days, would have been the sight of his horse munching next door's petunias. Now instead of having a horse, he's just equipped like one.

There are other ways of frustrating your milkman's amorous intentions:

• With your wife away on a trip to Manchester, invite your confused granny round and tell her to try on some of your wife's clothes to see whether she can still carry off the younger look. Finally leave instructions for her to open the bedroom window at exactly five past seven and to wave to the milkman down the road. Apparently it makes his day.

- Perform the same routine, but with you in your wife's clothes.

- Tip off the milkman's wife that he is up to no good at number 27.

- Appear in the bedroom doorway dressed as Jeremy Beadle.

And even if your milkman doesn't have the sex drive of a buck rabbit watching a Corrs video, you can still make his life hell.

7 MORE WAYS OF ANGERING YOUR MILKMAN

1. Set the dog on him.

2. Set your seven-year-old son on him.

3. Keep changing your milk order so he doesn't know whether he's coming or going.

4. Sneak out early in the morning and move everyone's milk, hiding it under bushes, on garage roofs, etc. The poor milkman will get the blame.

5. Pay him in pesetas left over from your holiday. Milkmen are in such a hurry that they never look at what you give them.

6. Leave abusive messages in your milk bottle.

7. If a neighbour has left a note out for the milkman, replace 'No potatoes this week, please' with something along the lines of 'Pop in and see me, big boy'. This will be particularly effective if your neighbour is over 80.

Girls and Boys

YOUR CHILDREN

Babies

Pregnancy is a pain for men. Women receive all the sympathy and support, yet it is men who have to put up with the wild mood swings, the fact that your partner looks like she's swallowed a beach ball and, of course, the decrease in sex from once a night to once a general election. In fact, men aren't really interested in the impending birth at all until they feel that first kick and immediately assume that their son is destined to be a professional footballer. It is a sobering thought that Julian Clary's father probably once came to the same conclusion.

In the run up to the birth it's all ante-natal classes, but these are no more a place for men than flower-arranging classes. All that stuff about cooking placenta. What's wrong with spaghetti bolognese? So give them a miss and go off down to the pub. If anything interesting happens, you can always spare five minutes to listen over breakfast, unless, of course, you've got a particularly heavy hangover.

You should make some effort to attend the birth, if only so that you can tell your partner how easy it looked. Still, if you're not careful you could find yourself suffering from a lack of sleep when the baby comes home because, for some reason, women get it into their head that the father should help with feeding and nappy-changing duties in the middle of the night. This is clearly preposterous, so you will need to arm yourself with a series of ready-made excuses.

8 REASONS WHY YOU CAN'T TEND TO THE BABY IN THE MIDDLE OF THE NIGHT

1. 'I've got an important meeting in the morning.'
2. 'I'm sure he called for "mummy".'
3. 'I only washed my hair last night – I don't want it messing up.'
4. 'You're so much better with him than me.'
5. 'Ooh, I've got cramp.'
6. 'I couldn't possibly face a nappy after that Indian takeaway.'
7. 'At times like this, he needs his mother.'
8. 'I'm asleep.'

As with a puppy, you can teach your baby all manner of tricks to ease the trauma of fatherhood. You can teach him to flick food at the walls, to rub the cat's fur up the wrong way, to poke his tongue out at the health visitor, to dig his nails in under mummy's, to tug the hairs in grandad's ears, to sink his tiny-but-deceptively-sharp teeth into Auntie Vi's nose when she bends down to kiss him and to say 'wanker' whenever anybody other than daddy walks into the room. These can be among the most rewarding moments in a proud father's life.

Young Children

For the first few years of their lives, children are so innocent they're crying out to be made to look stupid, which is why we give them names like Wayne and Kylie and dress them in bonnets, cardigans and bootees. Poor little sods – they probably think they'll have to spend the rest of their life in all-in-one babygros. And in little Anneka Rice's case, she was right.

As the infant's father, you are in a tremendous position of power, second only to that of its mother, two sets of grannies, two sets of grandads and assorted aunts and uncles. You will never be able to exert such influence at any other time in your life, certainly not at work where your expenses are queried on a weekly basis, nor with your wife who is still sleeping in the spare room 15 months after the birth. Whatever you tell your child at this stage will be treated as gospel. No arguments, no debates, just a cheerful gurgle in reply. So it's not a bad time to start laying down some ground rules and to put your offspring right about a few things in life.

14 FACTS THAT EVERY CHILD SHOULD BE TOLD BEFORE THE AGE OF EIGHT

1. Daddy is always right, even if he sometimes has to pretend that he is wrong, just to please mummy.
2. Daddy works hard all day at the office while mummy does bugger all.
3. If mummy's mummy had been born in the 12th century, she'd have been burned at the stake.
4. There is absolutely nothing wrong with daddies drinking to excess, but when mummies and grannies do, it's coarse and vulgar.
5. Ask mummy about anything to do with the birds and bees. She's the expert, having been round the block a few times.
6. Daddies must never be spoken to while there's football

on the telly.

7. Mummies can be interrupted at any time, day or night. That's their job.

8. Daddy may have a menial, poorly paid job, but that's only because he never had the opportunities you'll have.

9. Just because daddy can't programme the video doesn't mean he's not supremely intelligent.

10. Just because daddy's losing his hair doesn't mean he is getting old.

11. Just because daddy doesn't eat his cabbage doesn't mean you don't have to.

12. Mummy bosses daddy around because she's got an inferiority complex.

13. Father Christmas won't visit any child who draws faces on daddy while he's sleeping off an eight-pint session at the pub.

14. The grumpy neighbour who bangs on the wall when you're playing Deep Purple at three in the morning is the bogeyman.

Another amusing game to play is 'Confuse the Heath Visitor'. These worthy individuals, many of whom would make Boadicea look timid, conduct periodic visits to check on your child's progress. These are daunting occasions for the entire family, akin to being told that the Queen is in the neighbourhood and will be popping in for a cuppa in five minutes' time. Furthermore, Princess Margaret's with her and you're fresh out of gin. Having you as a father, your child will naturally be extremely bright and will therefore be eminently capable of deliberately leading the health visitor astray. So persuade him to get his colours wrong on purpose and to mix up the names of everyday objects. The health visitor will become extremely baffled when he repeatedly calls a cup a 'door' and a cat a 'house'. It may mean having your child taken into care for a few months, but it will be a good laugh.

Kids can be expensive, never more so than at Christmas. You could either try the traditional Scottish father's trick of telling his kids that mean Santa Claus has cancelled Christmas this year or buy presents that appeal to you. For example, tell your four-year-old daughter that you couldn't find any dolls in the toy shops so you bought her a Scalextric set instead, or a Black and Decker power drill.

And the drain on your wages gets even worse when they start school and need uniforms, bags and the like. Remembering how suffering at school turned out to be the making of you, offer a few useful pieces of advice to your child on his or her first day at Attila the Hun Infants.

9 THINGS TO TELL YOUR CHILD ON THEIR FIRST DAY AT SCHOOL

1. 'The teachers admire you if you answer them back. They expect you to challenge everything they say.'
2. 'The teachers like you to fight in the playground at break.'
3. 'You don't call your lady teachers "Ms", "Miss" or "Madam" but "Oi you".'
4. 'And the men teachers like to be called "Baldy".'
5. 'If you're missing mummy or daddy, just walk out of class.'

6. 'You don't bother with toilets at school – you just go in your desk.'

7. 'Now remember, the school bus is fondly known as Bertie and the school bike is Miss Wharton.'

8. 'Your first homework will be to bring home as many of the other children's satchels as you can.'

9. 'The teachers love the children to play practical jokes on them. Here's a banana skin to put in your classroom doorway.'

Young children can also be used as weapons to drive people around you to despair. This ploy works particularly well on public transport and nowhere better than on a train. Midweek trains are full of businessmen who like to sit in the aisle seat at a table and put their briefcase on the window seat. No matter how crowded the train gets and despite the fact that they haven't actually paid for two seats, they refuse to move their case to allow anybody else to sit down. Only when firmly pressed (preferably around the windpipe) will they grudgingly vacate the spare seat. They also love to spread their work right across the table, leaving the rest of you with nothing more than a tiny corner, but, if you are travelling with a small child, you can exact a full and gratifying revenge.

Lines such as 'Oi, mister, you've got a bogey hanging down' can be used as a warm up for all manner of terrorist tactics. Encourage your child to:

• Smear the businessman's papers or suit with a sticky lolly.

• Crayon the letter the businessman is writing.

- Spill squash on his important documents.

- Squirt him in the face with a water-pistol.

- Climb all over the table, scattering his work to all corners of the carriage.

- Force feed the businessman jelly babies.

- Generally talk in a loud, squawky voice.

It will take a true captain of industry to withstand such an onslaught, but a far more likely course of events is that the businessman will either move to another carriage or take early retirement.

Teenagers

Whilst young children can be manipulated against others, by the time they reach teenage years they have a nasty habit of turning on their masters. Having a teenager in the family is like discovering an old wartime bomb in the back garden – you never know when it's going to explode. Teenagers can be volatile, rude, moody, surly – and that's just on their more reasonable days. Since they are capable of making your life a misery with just a stare or a shrug of the shoulders, it is only fair that you should be able to get your own back from time to time.

33 FORMS OF REVENGE ON A TEENAGER

1. Tell your son it's perfectly OK for boys to wear short trousers to school at 13.

2. Tell your 13-year-old daughter that knitted balaclavas are the height of fashion this year.

3. Give them 50p a week pocket money and expect them to buy all of their clothes out of that.

4. Send them to boarding school.

5. Send them to military academy.

6. Insist on cutting your teenager's hair yourself with a pudding basin and a pair of rusty scissors, in order to save money. If he or she demands to go to a proper salon, deduct it from their meagre pocket money.

7. Tell your son you've had a letter from the school saying that everyone is to go in Seventies clothes on Monday. Pack him off in your old tank top and loon pants and wet yourself when he tells how he was jeered in the playground for being the only one not in school uniform.

8. Tell your son or daughter that you've had a letter from the Headmaster saying that school doesn't start until mid-day on Monday to allow for teacher training. Then laugh yourself silly when your offspring gets a detention for being three hours late.

9. Tell your son that you've had a letter from the school saying that the Headmaster wants to see him first thing on Monday morning to discuss his behaviour. Let him suffer all weekend before telling him on Monday morning that it was just your idea of a joke.

10. Apply mascara and lipstick to your son for school, telling him it's all the rage.

11. Comb your son's hair and straighten his tie as he is about to leave for school.

12. Tell your son that all girls go for a lad who buys his clothes at Millet's.

13. Tell your son that all girls expect you to try it on during a first date.

14. Tell your son that girls are always impressed by a boy who possesses the ability to fart, belch and puke.

15. Tell your son that girls often like to go to bingo on a first date.

16. Tell your daughter that a nice gentle drink for her to get used to alcohol is a treble scotch.

17. Tell your 14-year-old daughter that she certainly doesn't need a bra yet – she's got nothing to show.

18. Tell your 14-year-old daughter that she could do with losing some weight.

19. Give your daughter plastic surgery vouchers for her birthday.

20. Try to upstage your son in front of his girlfriend by wearing your tightest jeans and strongest aftershave.

21. Make a pass at your son's girlfriend, telling her that he's a waste of space and that she'd be much better off learning the ropes from a more mature man.

22. Tell your son that condoms should always be worn over the head.

23. Embarrass them in front of their friends by saying, 'Now you want to hear some real music' and putting on the Bay City Rollers.

24. Tell them about all the wild places where you had sex with their mother.

25. Tell them that everybody's doing the Twist at nightclubs these days.

26. Replace all their Michael Owen posters with monochrome photos of Tommy Lawton.

27. Dance ridiculously at their 18th birthday party.

28. Get embarrassingly drunk at their 18th birthday party.

29. Show their boyfriend/girlfriend photos of them as a baby and tell tales of their ability to fill a nappy.

30. Go out with them on dates.

31. Insist that they keep up membership of the Tufty Club even though they're 19.

32. Pop up from behind the sofa when they're involved in a heavy petting session, exclaiming 'Caught you!'

33. Try and look younger than them.

After Your Children Have Left Home

Just because your children are adults, have moved out and have lives of their own to lead, that is no reason why you shouldn't continue to haunt them and embarrass them at every opportunity. The secret is not to let them move too far away from you so that you can drop round unannounced on the pretence of 'just passing through on our way to Tesco's'. Even allowing for your wife's map-reading ability, this will not sound terribly convincing if you live in Norwich and your son or daughter lives in Manchester. If your grown-up children are wise to this and are determined to put as much distance as possible between themselves and you, all is still not lost. Either arrange for them to be sacked from work so that they can no longer afford to move or simply up sticks and follow them. Their joy will be unconfined when, two months after moving into a new property, they discover that you have moved in to a house just around the corner. 'You kept telling us what a lovely neighbourhood it was, so we thought we'd see if you were right.' This statement will serve to be doubly infuriating, not only because you won't let them escape, but also because it reaffirms the fact that only parents can judge whether something is right or wrong.

When calling round unexpectedly, be sure to vary your times so that there is absolutely no chance of your son or daughter being able to establish a routine. Breakfast or just before midnight are both good times for surprising newlyweds. You will, of course, need a steady supply of reasons for visiting at such unsociable hours, but with a sincere, yet determined delivery, the following will prove sufficiently credible:

- 'I'm painting the hall next week and I was saying to mother that the blue you've got in yours is too dark. I just wanted to confirm my suspicions.'

- 'Our television has broken down and there's a film on BBC2 which I particularly wanted to watch.'

- 'We've just had our holiday photos of Skegness back and we thought you'd like to see them. There's a particularly nice view of the clock tower and miniature railway.'

- 'I was wondering how that damp patch on your wall was.'

- 'We wondered whether you needed to borrow anything.'

- 'I've just heard that Bob Phillips – a chap I used to work with 25 years ago – has died. You've never met him, but we thought you'd like to know.'

- 'Just wanted to tell you about the putt I sank on the 16th this afternoon.'

- 'I expect you've heard about the bank robbery in the High Street this morning. Luckily, we were both a mile-and-a-half away at home at the time but we thought we'd better let you know that nobody tried to take us hostage or steal the Skoda for the getaway, just in case you were worried.'

Watching the Detectives

THE POLICE

Deliberately behaving badly in front of a police officer is one of the most stupid things you can do – on a par with slicing the end off your knob to see what it's like inside, playing Russian roulette with no empty chambers and asking your hairdresser for a Gary Lineker cut. The police don't always need an excuse to arrest you at the best of times, so goading them is asking for trouble. So if you are stopped in the street late at night, clearly the worse for wear, here are a few things it is best not to say:

- 'I'm not drunk – I'm casing that antique shop.'

- 'OK, so I've had seven pints. I'm not loitering – I'm just looking for my car.'

- 'Is that your truncheon or are you just pleased to see me?'

- 'This is a typical case of harassment by a fascist police force.'

- 'I know where you live.'

- 'Officer... I think I love you.'

- 'You'll never take me alive, copper.'

Nor on any account should you molest the officer's helmet, either by snatching it and playing football with it down the street or by using it as a receptacle for your vomit. Giving a false name is also frowned upon, but unless you come out with the Oriental 'U Fat Pig', it is unlikely to earn you a night in the cells. The most popular false names tend to be along the lines of Michael Mouse, Frederick Flintstone, Ronald McDonald and Rupert Bear. Ludwig van Beethoven does stand out a bit in Woking on a Friday night. For a change, use the seemingly innocuous Richard Head or Robert Sole. If you are asked to sign anything, simply scrawl 'Dick Head' and 'R. Sole'.

Apart from late-night revelry, the other occasion on which we are most likely to come into contact with the police is in our car should we somehow contrive to fall foul of a speed trap. When stopped by the police, it pays to be contrite. So if an officer orders you to pull over and asks, 'Do you know what speed you were doing?' do not reply:

- 'I have no idea, officer. I had my eyes closed.'

- 'Here's a tenner to forget all about it.'

- 'You're absolutely right officer, and I would also like 37 counts of armed robbery to be taken into consideration.'

- 'Which one's the speedometer?'

- 'No, who's in it?'

- 'Want to buy a camcorder for a fiver, no questions asked?

I've got 60 in the boot.'

- 'Could you hold my hip flask while I put on my glasses?'

- 'What do you mean, I can't do 35 in a 30 mph zone? Next you'll be telling me I need a licence.'

- 'I'm terribly sorry, officer. My guide dog usually barks if I'm driving too fast.'

- 'I don't know – the speedo doesn't work. What a crap car to nick. Ooops!'

Road to Nowhere

DRIVING TEST EXAMINERS

Driving examiners are not exactly renowned for their sense of humour. In fact, the only people less likely to see the funny side of a situation are a builder who's just dropped a 30lb mallet on his big toe, someone who has just seen his girlfriend run off with his best mate, and the entire German nation. Therefore any attempt at being jocular during your driving test will not only fall on stony ground, but also more than likely result in your failing. But what the heck?

21 WAYS TO ANNOY YOUR DRIVING TEST EXAMINER

1. Approach the car with a white stick and a guide dog.
2. When asked to read the licence plate of a nearby car, get out a pair of binoculars.
3. Pretend to be pissed by slurring your words and appearing unsteady on your feet.
4. Put the car stereo on and start singing away to the music.
5. Look in the mirror and comb your hair.
6. Ask him whether he fancies sharing a can of Foster's.
7. When a car cuts you up at a roundabout, leap out and threaten to throttle the driver.
8. Swear at every cyclist you come across.

9. Ask if you can stop off at a bank.

10. Scare the life out of an old lady on a pedestrian crossing by blasting your horn at her.

11. After stopping at a pedestrian crossing, make everyone run for their lives by revving your engine.

12. Disregard the examiner's directions and take a short cut you know.

13. Do the emergency stop when he is least expecting it and say, 'Just making sure you're still paying attention.'

14. Offer the examiner a night with your bird as a bribe.

15. Grip the examiner's knee tightly throughout the test.

16. Ask where the ejector seat is... just in case.

17. Offer your mum a lift.

18. Deliberately trap the examiner's tie in the door and refuse to release it until he tells you you've passed.

19. Lock him in the car until he passes you.

20. Tell him he'll be looking over his shoulder for the rest of his life unless he passes you.

21. Push him to the ground and call him a 'bent bastard' when he fails you.

Family Affair

YOUR IN-LAWS

When you first meet your future in-laws, you do more crawling than at the end of a night on the town. You go out of your way to assure the mother that you are a decent human being and that your intentions are strictly honourable, even though the moment she closes the front door in order to pop down to the corner shop for a packet of frozen peas, you are shagging her daughter something rotten on the new Axminster. You tell the mother that you drink only in moderation, have excellent job prospects and absolutely no sexual deviations. Basically, you lie through your teeth. And with the father, you agree that the Nuits St. Georges '73 is a much underrated vintage and express fascination in his collection of over 2,000 golf tees.

Only daughters are the toughest. If she's one of 12, she's just another one off the conveyor belt. Her parents have probably been through it all before and don't care as long as you don't display too many psychopathic tendencies over the table at Sunday tea. If your girlfriend is an only child, however, you come under closer scrutiny than you'd get from the KGB. There's more vetting than on *Animal Hospital*. Sometimes they just can't hide their disappointment that their daughter has chosen you. And to be fair, you have to see it from their point of view. It's not every mother's dream to acquire a pisshead for a son-in-law.

The alternative to the arse-lickey approach is the brutally honest, take-me-for-what-I-am strategy. By this, you don't give a toss what your in-laws think, but hope that they might eventually come to accept – and even perhaps admire – you for your disarming candour. Disciples of this method invariably resort to some of the following phrases:

14 THINGS WHICH MIGHT SOUR YOUR RELATIONSHIP WITH YOUR FUTURE MOTHER-IN-LAW

1. 'Your daughter goes like a train, doesn't she?'
2. 'Let's hope they're wrong about daughters growing to look like their mothers.'
3. 'Mind if I gob on your carpet?'
4. 'The cat kept staring at me so I fed it to the Dobermann next door.'
5. 'Haven't you lost weight? Only joking.'
6. 'Give me a break, you old bag.'
7. 'What crap wallpaper!'
8. 'Sorry about the stain on the sofa – that's our love juices from last night.'
9. 'Sorry if the noise from down here kept you awake last night, but you know what multiple orgasms are like. Looking at you, though, you probably don't.'
10. 'We couldn't get the fire to work so we set your armchair alight for a bit of warmth.'
11. 'Isn't that dress a bit low cut for someone your age?'
12. 'No wonder she wants to leave home with cooking like this!'
13. 'You'd be sacred in some countries.'
14. 'I've always had this fantasy about bedding mother and daughter.'

14 THINGS WHICH MIGHT OFFEND YOUR IN-LAWS AFTER MARRIAGE

1. 'She's mine now – you'll never see her again.'
2. 'Sorry, we're just off to a wife-swapping party.'
3. 'You'd really like her pimp – he's a good bloke.'
4. 'And to think she fell for all that crap I told her. You've got to laugh.'
5. 'I was just on the other line to my mistress.'
6. 'I'm not wasting good money on a house – we're going to squat instead.'
7. 'Do you know the number of a good abortionist?'
8. 'I've just discovered that nagging is hereditary.'
9. 'Didn't you know about my first three wives? They all died – in strange circumstances.'
10. 'I think I'm gay.'
11. 'I've packed her off to a religious commune.'
12. 'Grandchildren? You must be joking!'
13. 'Even after six years of marriage, she still gives me the horn.'
14. 'Hypothetically speaking, of course, if the pair of you were to be involved in a mysterious fatal accident tomorrow afternoon, how much, to the nearest pound, would your daughter get?'

10 THINGS TO DO WHEN YOUR IN-LAWS CALL ON YOU

1. Put a note on the door saying, 'Moved to Australia, 18/4/99. Will write.'
2. Hide behind the sofa and pretend you're out.
3. Go straight down the pub.
4. Answer the door wearing only your underpants and a smile.
5. Answer the door stark naked.
6. Join the Foreign Legion.
7. Call the police, saying someone's trying to break into your house.
8. Erect a remote-controlled guillotine over the front door.
9. Give your wife a sound knobbing while her parents sit sipping tea opposite.
10. Lend them your *Titanic* video, but substitute it with *Wagging Tongues – Lesbians on Heat*.

Money, Money, Money

TAXI DRIVERS

Cab drivers see us at our worst. Bevvied to the brim and topped up with Cantonese roast duck, we stagger into their world and beg them to take us home to an address we can barely pronounce. If they ask us to speak again – for further directions – they risk finding out just how tasty the Cantonese roast duck was first time round. Then again it's best to be pissed when you go for a ride in a cab. That way you can't see the meter flashing round and you don't have to listen to the driver droning on about politics, the World Cup, politics, the cost of living, politics, etc.

8 THINGS YOU'LL NEVER SEE IN A MINI-CAB

1. A meter which starts at anything near zero.
2. A car radio which makes anything other than a crackling noise.
3. A driver taking you the shortest way home.
4. A driver apologizing to a fellow motorist.
5. The vaguest adherence to any of the rules of the Highway Code.
6. A driver who says, 'I'm surprised the fare's that much.'
7. A driver with change for a fiver.
8. A driver saying 'goodnight' after you haven't given him a tip.

Mini-cab drivers almost expect you to chuck up in the back of their vehicle. Why else would they bother with soft seats, so conducive to the act of vomiting and in a material which retains the smell for weeks to come? Black cabs, on the other hand, have harsh, soulless plastic upholstery. They're not at all vomit-friendly. You may as well throw up in the gutter. In view of the state you're usually in when you call a cab, just about the worst thing you can do to the driver is breathe on him although those of a musical disposition could also stage a sing-song in the back. Now just because the driver is robbing you blind, there's no need for you to return the compliment. Running off without paying isn't funny... unless it's done with style. If there's a group of you, what you need to do is somehow acquire a shop window dummy. This may sound a tall order, but, after a few pints, anything is within your capabilities. Wedging the dummy between you in a reasonably upright position, climb into the cab and order your destination. From the driver's hazy view through the mirror, the dummy will simply be another glazed face in the back. The only reason it might stand out from the rest of you is because it's the only one that looks remotely sober. At the end of your journey, you all climb out in a hurry, leaving the dummy behind and telling the driver, 'He'll pay.' By the time the driver realizes what's happened, you'll have disappeared into the night. Of course, you could try this with an inflatable doll but that would mean parting with an exquisite piece of craftsmanship and a faithful friend.

You Woke Up The Neighbourhood

YOUR NEIGHBOURS

If only life were like Ramsey Street. People popping into each other's houses to chat, snog, land jobs, have parties, jump to the wrong conclusions and then, when you move away, all the neighbours throw a giant farewell bash for you and turn out to wave you off. In reality, neighbours are more likely to pop into each other's houses to nick the video recorder, and as for the leaving do, it's usually one '*bon voyage*' card and plenty of dark mutterings about 'Thank God he's moving'.

By rights, you should treat your neighbours the way you would wish them to treat you, but that's a boring old philosophy. Unless you happen to fancy your neighbours, a much sounder proposition is to treat them as badly as possible, but don't let them know you were responsible.

8 ANONYMOUS TRICKS TO PLAY ON YOUR NEIGHBOURS

1. Stick a leaflet through their letter-box telling them that if they turn up at the travel agent's in the High Street at 11am on Saturday morning dressed in a lion's costume, they will win a safari holiday for two in Kenya.
2. Phone the Monster Raving Looney Party and arrange a home recruitment visit for your elderly neighbours.

3. Empty the contents of their wheelie bin on their drive. After all, the binmen do much the same.

4. Arrange for them to be sent a stack of literature about piles. You could try a pile of literature about stacks, but somehow it's not as effective.

5. Pour water on their drive on a frosty night so that it becomes a skating rink by morning.

6. Creep out and pinch the newspaper from their letter-box every morning.

7. Put a promotion through their door promising that any couple who tango across Market Square on Saturday morning will win £100.

8. Spray 'Bastard' on their garage door (this is only in extreme cases of neighbour wars).

Alternatively you can adopt the persona of the neighbour from hell by:

- Deliberately setting off your car alarm late at night.

- Revving up your car early in the morning.

- Wheeling your bin out noisily at midnight.

- Turning your music up loud.

- Staging wild, all-night parties. If your neighbour comes round to complain, make sure the door is answered by the girl with fewest clothes on.

- If your neighbours are particularly prudish, instead of decorating the tree in your front garden with fairy lights, dangle old bras and knickers from the branches.

If you are fortunate enough to be madly in love with your neighbour, your approach will be somewhat different. Alas, the result will probably still be the same in that, despite your best intentions, she'll still find you an annoying little prat. Winning over a girl who clearly has about as much interest in you as your granny has in learning to hang-glide, is one of the greatest challenges a bloke can face. Remeber though that a faint heart never won my fair lady – although quite what Audrey Hepburn's got to do with it is a puzzle – so you mustn't allow yourself to become downhearted by things like total and utter rejection. Just because she says she would rather go out with Jack the Ripper doesn't necessarily constitute a 'no'.

To have any chance of working your way into her affections, you will need to learn all there is to know about her lifestyle. Binoculars, or, if necessary, a telescope, trained on her bedroom will do for starters, but to get on the right scent and acquire a real sense of proximity, you may feel the urge to help yourself to a pair of knickers from her washing line... purely in the course of furthering spiritual understanding. You can try conveying your feelings via anything from signwriters in the sky to scrawling terms of endearment on her copy of the *Daily Mail* as it sits in her letter-box, but you can't beat physical contact. And for that, you need to worm your way into her flat, ideally at a time when she is in skimpy black lingerie.

8 REASONS TO GIVE FOR CALLING UNEXPECTEDLY ON THE GIRL NEXT DOOR

1. 'I heard a thud and wanted to make sure you were all right.'

2. 'There's supposed to be a prowler about – they've dubbed him the Beast of Balham. No, the Terror of Tooting's been caught. And the Monster of Mitcham turned out to be 89 with a gammy leg.'

3. 'It's a proven statistic that 81 per cent of women who are attacked spend the night alone.'

4. 'I'll sleep on the sofa and pretend to be a guard dog. You won't even know I'm here – except of course when I bark and growl every hour on the hour.'

5. 'Can I borrow some corn flakes?'

6. 'I heard Jehovah's Witnesses were on the loose in the neighbourhood.'

7. 'I could wallpaper your bedroom. It's easier to do it at night. You don't get distracted by Richard and Judy.'

8. 'I'm a very keen astronomer and there's a better view of the Plough from your flat. In fact on a clear night, you can see the Rose and Crown as well.'

In a Big Country

FOREIGN TOURISTS

For the purposes of feeding mis-information, there are no easier victims than foreign tourists. After all, they've already been tricked once by whoever told them that London was worth visiting. So if a couple approach you, guide-book in hand and with a glazed look on their faces, offer them the benefit of your local knowledge to ensure that they have a holiday in Britain which they'll never forget.

21 THINGS TO TELL FOREIGN TOURISTS

1. The cheapest way to travel around London is by taxi. Just tell the driver you're an overseas tourist and he'll give you a discount.
2. The most popular nudist beach in Britain is at Budleigh Salterton.
3. You can park anywhere you see yellow lines along the side of the road.
4. The prettiest place in Britain is Castleford in West Yorkshire.
5. The best bargains to be had in London are from the gift stalls along Oxford Street.
6. Every county in England drives on the left except Surrey.
7. Underground travel is free for foreign tourists. You just climb over the little barriers.

8. If you want to post a letter, leave it in the black plastic bags which line the street in the morning.

9. The most romantic spot in London is around the back of King's Cross station at night.

10. The official form of greeting to anyone from Liverpool is 'thieving Scouse git'.

11. The quickest way to get from London to Windsor is via Birmingham.

12. The Prime Minister's residence has moved from Downing Street to Camden Town.

13. Nightclub bouncers are gay. They love to be chatted up.

14. On pedestrian crossings, the red man means go and the green man means wait.

15. When you see a traffic warden, it is an old English custom to spit in their face.

16. The M25 is hardly ever busy.

17. The cheapest places in London for drinks are Soho strip clubs.

18. If you see a shop saying 'Butcher', it means that it sells fruit and vegetables.

19. Street crime in London is very rare. You can walk through Brixton at night with your wallet open without any fear of it being snatched.

20. The Queen always goes for a dawn stroll down the Old Kent Road. Get there early if you want to see her.

21. A London policeman enjoys nothing more than being given a playful kick on the ankle.

Son of my Father

YOUR PARENTS

Parents are easily shockable. No matter how hard they try to be trendy and keep up to date with modern fads, they can never quite help being a generation removed. Life simply moves too quickly for them. They'll attempt to maintain some sort of dialogue with you by going out and buying CDs by Oasis and The Manic Street Preachers, only to find that a few months later the charts are filled by acts they've never heard of. Then they get frustrated and it all comes pouring out during an edition of Top of the Pops when they moan that all modern music is rubbish and that there's never been anything worth listening to since Herman's Hermits and Freddie and the Dreamers were in their prime.

Other parents don't even try to understand their sons. They occupy the moral high ground and dismiss anything that has occurred since 1955 as decadent, including the hula-hoop, decimalization and Bobby Crush. Naturally, as opera buffs, their principal complaint about rock music is that they can't make out the words. In the circumstances, hardly a day goes by without you incurring their displeasure one way or another, whether it's your hair, your clothes or the fact that you've made half the street pregnant. So why bother trying to please them? You might just as well wind them up even more.

25 WAYS OF SHOCKING YOUR PARENTS

1. Come home from college with fake tattoos on either arm. Obviously your parents will think these are real. Own up before they write you out of their will.

2. Tell Jerry Springer you were abused as a child.

3. Announce that you're leaving college to join a hippie sect.

4. If they haven't seen your girlfriend for a few weeks, get her to arrive with a cushion stuffed up her jumper.

5. If they haven't seen your girlfriend for a few months, get her to arrive pushing a pram.

6. Offer them a joint.

7. Tell your mum that while she was out, a police officer knocked on the door to report that dad's car had been seen in a red light district.

8. Ask for a packet of condoms for your 14th birthday.

9. Take down the posters of Louise from your bedroom wall and put up lots of George Michael posters instead.

10. Proudly show off your new pierced navel. You can tell them it's a fake after letting them suffer for three days.

11. After your girlfriend has stayed over, leave a pregnancy testing kit in the bathroom.

12. Leave an empty bottle of meths on your bedside table with a meths-soaked glass next to it.

13. Tell your mum that while she was out a strange woman rang up for dad, but put the phone down in a hurry.

14. Tell your dad that while he and mum were out shopping a strange man called for mum with a bunch of flowers. He looked embarrassed when he realized she wasn't in.

15. Go round to your local off licence and ask the manager for some empty vodka, gin or whisky bottles. Stash them under your bed or in drawers – somewhere your mum is sure to stumble across them.

16. Come from college with a fake scar down your cheek, saying you don't want to talk about how you got it.

17. Have your hair styled in a replica of the Millennium Dome.

18. Announce that you've joined the Animal Liberation Front and begin by setting the hamster free.

19. Bandage your right ear, douse it in ketchup and say you've sliced it off so you can get as good an art report as Van Gogh.

20. Get a book about gonorrhoea from the library and leave it on your bed so that your mum will find it.

21. Get a book about gymslip pregnancies from the library and leave that on your bed where your mum will find it.

22. Use the book token that Auntie Rene sent you for your birthday to buy *The Joy of Sex*.

23. Say that you've got a job as a rent boy... sorry, rent man.

24. Come home one day with your girlfriend and pretend that you've got married.

25. Say that from now on you would prefer to be known as Shirley and are currently saving up for the operation.

Instead of deliberately behaving badly, you can annoy your parents just as much by pretending to have become a religious zealot. Denounce golf clubs as the tools of the Devil, whist as a wicked sin and damn everything else which they hold dear. Switch off *The Antiques Roadshow* on the grounds that it is peddling greed, that Hugh Scully is Beelzebub incarnate, and that anyone who watches will rot in hell. For good measure, threaten to run the Lord's sword through Mrs Hitchens next door for doing her washing on the Sabbath.

Of all the things you can do to upset your parents, however, arguably the most damaging is to saddle them with a potentially unsuitable daughter-in-law. Precisely what constitutes such a being depends to which stratum of society your parents belong.

Unsuitable Girlfriends to Bring Home

Upper-Class Parents

1. A girl who works for a living.
2. Bianca off *EastEnders*.
3. Anyone called Kylie.
4. A girl who prefers Tennants Extra to Earl Grey.
5. Anyone carrying a Woolworth's bag.
6. Anyone who didn't study Latin at school.

Middle-Class Parents

1. A girl covered from head to toe in tattoos.
2. A girl who rolls her own.
3. A girl who cheerfully reveals all the different places she's had sex and then runs her hands lovingly over your parents' dinner table.

4. A girl who swears like a trooper.

5. A girl with pierced lips and a row of nose studs.

6. A Page Three girl.

7. A girl with a bigger car than your dad.

Working-Class Parents

1. Tara Palmer-Tomkinson.

2. Anyone called Fiona.

3. A girl who prefers Earl Grey to Tennants Extra.

4. A girl who likes ponies – unless they're pit ponies.

5. Anyone carrying a Harrods shopping bag.

6. Anyone who did study Latin at school.

Gonna Make You an Offer You Can't Refuse

HOUSE BUYERS

The decision to sell your house is usually a joint one, but there are times when your partner wants to move and you don't. She might be fed up with the scruffy pubs, the tandoori takeaways and the private shops which, conversely, are the very things which attracted you to the area in the first place. So while she is eager to sell up to the first buyer, you have no intention whatsoever of moving. You daren't tell her that to her face, of course, for fear of getting the silent treatment or being branded with a red-hot iron, so you make a pretence of going along with the plans to sell. All the while, however, you are plotting to sabotage the sale.

There are any number of things you can do in advance to deter would-be buyers. While your partner is running round making the place look tidy, you are cunningly undoing all her good work. Follow her round, drop sweet wrappers here and there, hide an empty lager can under the cushion of the sofa the buyers are going to sit on, add a few black fingerprints to the pale walls, tear off a strip of wallpaper – it will all help make the place look a dump. Pay particular attention to the kitchen and bathroom – the two rooms in which the woman, the one who inevitably has the final say, places the most importance.

Few women want to move into a kitchen which looks as if it's just staged the first Food Olympics. Unscrew one of the door handles so that it comes away in the buyer's hands while they are looking round, loosen a few tiles on the kitchen wall so that when you bang it to show how solid the foundations are, they come crashing down and arrange a mini-disaster by putting in duff fuses so that the wiring appears dodgy. Finally, don't neglect yourself. Your partner may look nicely scrubbed, but there's no need for you to follow suit. Put on your tattiest T-shirt and the jeans with the holes in the knees and the crotch. As a finishing touch, douse yourself liberally with TCP. Nobody will want to hang around for too long.

If none of these moves work, try the verbal touch.

16 THINGS TO SAY TO PUT OFF POTENTIAL HOUSE BUYERS

1. 'You'd never know this house was built on an old burial ground, would you?'

2. 'Can you smell gas? Sorry, it's a constant problem in this place.'

3. 'I always think damp gives a house character.'

4. 'We hardly ever hear the neighbours – but then most of the family are doing time in Brixton for GBH.'

5. 'Did the estate agent mention the woman who was brutally murdered in the second bedroom 12 years ago?'

6. 'I think people exaggerate the problem of subsidence. We've only had two landslips this year. Admittedly we lost the dog in one...'

7. 'They say the water is OK to drink, but we buy bottled to be on the safe side.'

8. 'Whatever you do, don't leave your car outside around here.'

9. 'Terrible news about the interest rates, isn't it?'

10. 'The cat is really sorry to be moving – there are so many mice to feed on.'

11. 'The windows don't fit very well, but although you get a terrific draught blowing through, at least it means there's not much condensation.'

12. 'It's fairly quiet at night – apart from the bloke over the road and his pneumatic drill.'

13. 'The walls are rock solid most of the time. Just don't try and put up any shelves.'

14. 'We've had so many break-ins, we just felt it was time to get out.'

15. 'You know about the multi-storey car park they're building at the end of the garden, do you?'

16. 'It will be such a relief if we can sell this place. The estate agent told us we'd be hard pushed to give it away.'

Radio Gaga

DISC JOCKEYS

You're nobody until you've been on local radio. And if you haven't been on yet, it's probably just an oversight. With so much airtime to fill each week and only so much of interest in any one region, it is hardly surprising that some local radio stations get pretty desperate. In between playing Nana Mouskouri's back catalogue, they resort to interviewing anybody local with something to sell – be it a book or a pound of tomatoes – and anyone in the region who has even tenuous connections with a national story. Your cousin once met somebody who used to live near Bill Clinton as a kid? That will do nicely.

Should you be invited to be a guest on local radio, there are various ways of ruffling the presenter's feathers. You could try barging into the studio while he is reading the news and start chatting to him noisily. Remarks such as, 'I hear you got well pissed last night,' will provide an appropriate interlude to a story about drink driving. Or you may prefer pulling faces at him while he is reading a particularly serious item; switching his easy listening CD for 'Je T'Aime...'; playing with his knobs; doing the entire interview with a paper bag over your head; or yelling into the microphone so that everyone in the region's distant outposts can hear you.

Most local radio interviews are live which gives the guest the opportunity to be outrageous on air, to achieve that 15 seconds of fame before the presenter wakes up, realises what is going on, switches off the microphone and slips on "Till The White Rose Blooms Again"... again.

22 THINGS TO SLIP INTO A LOCAL RADIO INTERVIEW ABOUT PROTECTING CHRYSANTHEMUMS IN WINTER

1. A passage from *Mein Kampf*.
2. The words 'Coitus interruptus'.
3. Animal noises.
4. A plea for your wife to come back.
5. A tirade against Peter Mandelson.
6. A celebration of the vocabulary of Stanley Unwin.
7. The word 'vulture' at the end of each sentence.
8. A savage attack on the way Alan Titchmarsh treats runner beans.
9. Lincoln's Gettysburg Address.
10. A demand for the return of your video recorder.
11. A review of *Blind Date*.
12. 'Happy birthday, Auntie Win'.
13. A commercial for Brain's faggots.
14. An impersonation of Daffy Duck.
15. The chorus of "Una Paloma Blanca".
16. A demand that the traffic warden who patrols Park Street be strung up from the nearest lamp-post.
17. A detailed account of the mating habits of the African elephant. (You may be cut off at 'when you see the elephant's erection and think it's going to charge, content yourself with the thought that most women would be only too happy to pay.')
18. A detailed account of the mating habits of the show's producer.

19. An appeal on behalf of football referees with poor eyesight.

20. An excerpt from *Noddy Goes to the Seaside*.

21. A denunciation of General Pinochet.

22. A limerick beginning, 'There was a young woman called Annie.'

Help the Aged

WRINKLIES

Old people need no help in the art of behaving badly. It seems to be second nature to them, in the same way that your cat will always choose the shirt you were going to wear for work on which to regurgitate a bowl of beef Whiskas. To see a prickly pensioner in action is to understand why the Germans never stood a chance. Whether it be elbowing their way into the Post Office queue or bodily removing a heavily pregnant woman who has unwittingly sat in the bus seat reserved for the elderly, they represent a formidable foe. They are also utterly predictable and have a selection of set complaints which they can use to fit any occasion. Among them are:

- 'I can remember when all this was fields.'

- '37p? What's that in proper money?'

- 'I didn't fight in the war to support the likes of them.'

- 'Kids today don't know how lucky they are.'

- 'There was none of this when I was a lad.'

- 'Some of the kids today, you can't tell whether they're boys or girls.'

- 'They've got no respect, that's their trouble.'

- 'You can't call that music! It's just a racket!'

- 'A ball and a top that's all we ever got for Christmas. And we were grateful.'

- 'In my day, you could go all the way to London on the tram for 2d.'

- 'They should bring back National Service.'

- 'They should bring back hanging.'

- 'They should bring back the birch.'

- 'They should bring back trial by ordeal.'

- 'They should bring back Arthur Askey.'

Wrinklies enjoy nothing more than moaning about the youth of today – anyone under 50 qualifies as a youth in their eyes – and therefore you should make every effort to confirm their prejudices. Attaching a rocket to their stair-lift so that they can cover ground to first-floor landing in 0.000000001 seconds or inserting a Mercedes Formula One engine into their mobility carriage is probably taking things a bit far, but you can wind them up equally effectively just with a word or two in the right place. So next time you go to the pub, seek out a pair of old codgers and sit down within earshot. If they happen to be regulars, you can get in early and pinch their seats, a move which will earn you a piercing glare capable of putting Darth Vader to flight and ensure disapproval of whatever you say.

If they're women, go into graphic detail about sex, relating an imaginary encounter containing all manner of deviations. They'll be listening intently and tut-tutting away, their faces as sour as the plastic lemons on their hats. By the time you get to 'I'd never seen a vicar in that sort of dog collar', they'll probably decide to move. If they're men, sound off about how football in the fifties was rubbish and how Matthews and Finney would have struggled to get into Darlington's team today. Such statements will prompt a fiery backlash and, if you're really lucky, maybe even a 'flogging's too good for them'.

These bus-pass bullies are firm believers in positive action. For example, if you heard that the local greengrocer had been charged with living off immoral earnings, you'd either ask him for a few names and addresses or you might decide to take your custom elsewhere, but a wrinkly would march straight down to the shop, tell him what he could do with his parsnips and whack him over the head with her umbrella. This admirable – and thoroughly entertaining trait – can be turned to your advantage by dropping malicious rumours into the right ears. Try any of the following:

- Councillor Richardson is an advocate of compulsory euthanasia for the over 65s.

- The man at number six is a cannibal.

- Rationing is being re-introduced next month. You can pick up your book at the Post Office.

- They're planning to knock down the sheltered accommodation off the High Street to make way for a new Asda.

- The government are planning to put VAT on dentures. If you feel strongly about this, write to your local paper.

- Old-age pensions are being abolished from next January.

- The Japanese are poised to invade. If you see any about, either make a citizen's arrest or report them to your nearest police station.

- Mrs Baxter at number 33 is on the game.

- From Friday, anyone driving a mobility carriage must wear a crash helmet.

Steamy Windows

DOUBLE-GLAZING SALESMEN

Door-to-door salesmen are a breed apart. Whether they're selling dusters or God, they have a skin thicker than that of a rhinoceros. As a result, they are immune to normal human emotions such as despondency, humility and honesty. At the top of the salesman tree – a mere sheepskin jacket above the used-car vendor – is the double-glazing salesman.

The double-glazing salesman used to be a frequent visitor to urban houses and gardens all the year round, but the use of pesticides has hit numbers badly. It has become a shy, secretive creature, preferring to operate over the phone where its song of 'UPVC' rings out across the land on summer evenings. However, when it is lured out into the open by a customer's expression of interest, it can still be seen in its finest plumage. And there are still a few areas where it can be spotted scurrying up driveways and back down again 30 seconds later, carrying a clipboard and a colour brochure in the hope of feathering its nest.

A double-glazing salesman will do almost anything to secure a sale. This includes soaking himself in aftershave immediately prior to setting foot in your house, putting on a cheesey grin and agreeing with whatever you say. This entry into 'Uriah Heep mode' gives you the upper hand. Test his commitment to a sale by seeing whether he agrees with any of the following:

- 'Your aftershave makes the place smell like a brothel.'

- 'The last time I saw a haircut like that was in Henry V.'

- 'Your tie's crap.'

- 'Millwall are better than Chelsea.'

- 'Don't you walk funny?'

- 'My dad could beat up your dad.'

- 'You salesmen are all wankers.'

- 'Sporty is the best-looking Spice Girl.' (A true test since only Sporty's dad, Stevie Wonder and a double-glazing salesman are likely to agree).

- 'Your product is horribly over-priced.'

- 'You'd like to shag my girlfriend, wouldn't you?'

This last question provides your get-out clause: if he says 'yes', it gives you an excuse to throw him out of the house and threaten to report him; if he says 'no', you can claim that he's just insulted your girlfriend; if he says 'no' then quickly changes his mind to 'yes', you throw him out of the house and threaten to report him; if, on the other hand, he says, 'Too late, mate, been there, done that,' you can throw them both out of the house.

Rather than test his resolve, you may just like to string him along for a couple of hours. Maybe there's nothing much on the telly, or you're feeling in a particularly sadistic frame of mind. Let him get out all his brochures and give you the company spiel and then when you've got bored, tell him you've changed your mind – you don't think you'll bother with new double-glazing after all.

However the really persistent salesman won't give up that easily and will still be there at dawn if he thinks he's in with a chance. So you may need to come up with more persuasive reasons as to why he should leave.

- 'Because I will personally rip your tape measure to shreds if you don't.'

- 'There's been a spate of late-night car thefts in the area.'

- 'We're expecting the neighbours around for a drink.' (Beware: this may merely encourage him to stay and try and sell them double-glazing, too.)

- 'My girlfriend's gagging for it.' (Beware: potentially similar problem to above.)

- 'I can hear our cat coming in and the last salesman we had here, it went for his throat.'

- 'I'm a serial killer.'

- 'Jehovah's Witnesses are about.'

Killer Queen

MEETING ROYALTY

Behaving badly in front of royalty has proved a costly business down the centuries. At best, you get a few months in the Tower Hotel; at worst you wake up in the morning to discover that your body ends at your neck. With the exception of Ethelred the Unready, the Queen is just about the last person you'd want to make fun of. You'd be better advised making fun of a High Court judge or an axe murderer than Her Maj. So, as much as anything, it is for the continued health and well being of her subjects that strict protocol should be observed at all times when being introduced to the Queen. For example, it would be frowned upon to:

- Try and knock her hat off.

- Try and knock her crown off.

- Wipe your oily hands on her coat.

- Call her 'toots'.

- Call her 'darling'.

- Knee her playfully in the groin.

- Try her gloves on.

- Give her a Chinese burn.

- Snog her. Similarly, there are certain things one ought never really to say to the Queen. These include:

- 'My mum's got that dress.'

- 'Do you and Phil still do the business?'

- 'Got any Rizlas?'

- 'Oi, tich, out of the way, the Queen's expected any minute.'

- 'I hate bloody corgis.'

- 'Blimey! Have you been eating garlic?'

- 'Whatever made you marry that guy?'

- 'I bet you wish you lived somewhere smaller.'

- 'I bet you always have to hide the gin when your sister comes round.'

- 'Vive la Republique!'

- 'You look better on your stamps.'

- 'What's your favourite position?'

- 'Kids! They're nothing but trouble, eh?'

- 'You couldn't lend us a quid, could you?'

- 'I've got all your albums.'

Devil in Diguise

YOUR BOSS

It's either a brave man or one who's got another job lined up that deliberately behaves badly in front of his boss. On the day you leave – once you're sure that he's put into your collection – you can hit him with a few home truths which you've been storing up for the past seven years.

- 'We all know it's a glass eye.'

- 'We all know your trips to the dentist are really to Kinky Katie who operates out of a third-floor flat in Soho.'

- 'There's one thing I've always meant to ask you. Do you and Bob Geldof share the same tailor?'

- 'We all know you've only kept your job because you're shagging the MD's secretary.'

- 'No wonder your wife has been putting it about.'

If you're past the stage of caring, take the opportunity to show up your boss at an important presentation. Sabotage his speech, either by replacing his neatly typed script with blank pages, or by inserting a few words of your own. Any Brownie points he earns by welcoming the company's new Japanese partners to Britain will be lost when he goes on to describe them as 'a plague from the East'. If he survives that, he will surely perish on his announcement that Miss Watkins has been promoted to personnel manager 'not only because of her diligence and efficiency, but also, because in my opinion, she is the best lay in the entire company'.

Speech doctoring is equally effective if your company conveys messages to the staff via closed-circuit television. By sneaking in and changing the computer text, you can relay all manner of useful information to the building.

- For a one-night stand, no strings, no questions asked, phone Jane in petty cash, ext. 2310.

- Wanted urgently: morning-after pill. Phone Lynn (Mr Rickett's secretary) on ext. 2556.

- Happy birthday to Mrs Williamson in the canteen – 58 and still as ugly as ever.

- Did you know that John in goods inwards is still shagging Marilyn in accounts even though his wife's pregnant? A well-wisher.

- Are you a cross-dresser? Don't be shy. Give Keith in maintenance a call on ext. 2141.

- For sale: half-full jar of haemorrhoid cream. Ring Norman in the press office on ext. 2080.

- If anyone can remember shagging me at Rachel's leaving do last week, please, please, please give me a call. Janice on ext. 2779.

- To Tim in sales. Where were you last night, you bastard? Your wife.

- Do you need lessons in fiddling your expenses? Just ask Brian on ext. 2321.

- Are you interested in recently acquired television sets, as featured on *Crimestoppers*? See Eric the electrician.

- Warning: Don't go out with Kevin in security unless you want a dose of the clap. Marie, accounts.

- What's it like with a donkey? Ask Simone in personnel. And she's got the photos to prove it!!! For more conventional holiday snaps of the company outing to Blackpool, see Mrs Gittins in duplicating.

- Congratulations to Joan and Dave Bartrop on their silver wedding anniversary. Joan obviously turns a blind eye to the fact that Dave's been shafting Yvette from the mailing room. Or perhaps she doesn't know...

- The press office drinking club meets every Friday afternoon at four o'clock, provided Mr Mackintosh is away. Discreet outsiders welcome. Bring bottle.

- Lost: a pair of M&S lilac knickers and matching bra behind the sofa in the bar. Anyone finding them, please ring Lucy on the reception desk on ext. 2000.

- Call Ray on ext. 2643 for the biggest collection of porno mags in the company. Just in! Tit and bum shots of Sandra in accounts. Plus... the eagerly awaited video of Mrs Braithwaite from the catering department going down on Ron the van driver at the office party!!!

If your boss is doing an illustrated presentation complete with projector, instead of tampering with his speech, you could swap around some of his slides. A nice photocopy of your bum magnified on screen will liven up his talk no end. Since he is your head of department, you are also in a position to embarrass him acutely at the post-presentation drinks. You could either get completely rat-arsed (although this isn't always easy on warm Liebfraumilch) or simply pretend to be. Start slobbering all over the MD's wife, put your hand on a few pairs of nicely rounded buttocks, tip up the tray of food in protest that there are no cheese and pickle sandwiches and pass on a few indiscretions about your boss.

4 THINGS TO TELL THE MANAGING DIRECTOR'S WIFE ABOUT YOUR BOSS

1. 'He's after your husband's job.'
2. 'He's after you.'
3. 'Somebody should keep an eye on his expenses.'
4. 'You remember that lovely brown dress you wore to the company open day? He said you looked like a sack of potatoes in it.'

On the other hand, if you're quite keen to hold on to your job, you will have to act anonymously. Try sending him stuff through the post – a blackmail note with letters cut out from newspapers, threatening to expose his liaison with Miss Figgis; a letter supposedly from a rival company offering him a hush-hush job in Barbados at a salary of £150,000 a year; or a fake memo from the MD rewarding him for all his efforts with a week's extra holiday as from Monday – when he doesn't turn up for work, questions will be asked.

The other time to strike is when the boss is away. In his absence, everyone takes turns at sitting in his chair and the entire office recaptures that playground mentality. Try staging your own Office Olympics:

- *Soccer.* A penalty shoot-out competition with a ball made from paper and sellotape, using the boss's cupboards as the goal.

- *Hurdles.* Build a course round the office of boxes, waste-paper bins and humans.

- *Equestrian events*: The secretary climbs on your back and rides you round the course. The fastest time wins. This is often worth playing twice.

- *Shot putt*: Throwing the boss's paper weight. Breakage results in disqualification.

- *High jump*: Vaulting over the boss's desk.

- *Archery*: Use rubber bands to fire paper clips at a suitable target on the wall, such as a photo of the boss at an awards ceremony. The winner is the first to hit him between the eyes.

- *Hoop-la*: A new Olympic sport requiring a reel of sellotape to be lobbed over a waste-paper spike.

- *Javelin*: Throwing the umbrella.

- *Wrestling*: A compulsory event, particularly if there are two lesbians in your office. Keep the camcorder handy.

- *Marathon*: The fastest to eat a Snickers bar.

5 MORE OFFICE ACTIVITIES FOR WHEN THE BOSS IS AWAY

1. Forge his signature and order more booze for the drinks cabinet.
2. Have a picnic on the carpet.
3. Do something unmentionable in his 'out' tray.
4. Have sex in his chair. When he comes back, you can snigger to yourself every time he sits down.
5. Get in early on the morning your boss is due back from holiday and tie each other to chairs. When the boss arrives, tell him you've all been left bound and gagged over the weekend by masked raiders. He'll give you the rest of the week off.

My Sweet Lord

THE VICAR

Vicars aren't what they used to be. Ever since the Joy Strings appeared on the *Val Doonican Show* in the Sixties, spearheading the Salvation Army's assault on the charts with an attempt to prove that the tambourine could be as exciting a rock innovation as the electric guitar and the synthesizer, religion has gone all trendy. The days when vicars all looked like Alastair Sim and ate cucumber sandwiches are long gone. Now the younger ones look like the Gallagher brothers and appear more likely to favour a knuckle sandwich. Some are rougher than their parishioners. They haven't just got the courage of their convictions, they've actually got the convictions.

Fortunately there are still some of the old school vicars about and it is they who should be the targets for your bad behaviour. After all, the trendy vicars would just join in. So, if the vicar should call round for afternoon tea in the course of collecting your girlfriend's unwanted Cliff Richard CD, don't treat him any differently from any other visitor. It's how the Church would want it.

15 THINGS TO DO IN FRONT OF THE VICAR

1. Put on a Jesus mask.

2. Put on a Glenn Hoddle mask.

3. Sit there in your underpants.

4. Fart loudly at every opportunity, followed by the traditional, 'Sorry, vicar.'

5. Ask him whether he wants to buy any cheap hymn books.

6. An impression of Rev Ian Paisley.

7. Cut your toe nails on to the carpet.

8. Pretend to sneeze in his cup.

9. Suggest a game of Twister with him and your girlfriend.

10. Suggest a game of strip I-Spy.

11. Tell him the joke about the nun and the soap.

12. Keep a straight face when he tells you that people still flock to see his organ.

13. Read *Forum* inside a copy of *Satanic Verses*.

14. Read *Satanic Verses* inside a copy of *Forum*.

Guaranteed to break the ice on any occasion are a selection of lad's lists. As well as encouraging reasoned debate, these frequently have the added benefit of giving you a hard-on. So why not ask the vicar to name in order the five television weathergirls he thinks have got the best arse or, to appeal closer to home, the five all-time *Songs of Praise* presenters who look like they're up for it. If he is able to answer from first-hand experience, you may have more in common than you thought. Other suitable topics for debate include:

• The top-five girl singers with the best jugs.

• The top-five cashiers in Barclays you'd most like to shag.

• Your top-five BBC blondes.

• The top-five positions for doing it with Liz Hurley.

If, by some mistake, the topic of conversation should get on to religion, the vicar may ask you what you would pray for. On no account should you answer with any of the following:

- A bigger weapon.

- Your girlfriend to turn into Louise Lombard.

- A security van to stop outside your house with the back doors open.

- Your next-door neighbour to be attacked by a plague of locusts.

- Anglia Water to replace tap water with lager.

- A cure for brewer's droop.

- Your boss to be run over by a number 46 bus.

- His successor to be Samantha Janus.

- Lucky Rascal to win the 3.30 at Haydock.

- The girl in the building society to drop them.

- 'Piss off and let me watch *Neighbours*.'

Is She Really Going Out With Him?

YOUR EX-GIRLFRIEND

Revenge is petty, vindictive and juvenile, but it can also be bloody good fun and, in the case of exacting retribution on a girlfriend who has heartlessly dumped you, absolutely essential. So bollocks to all that stuff about rising above it, keeping your dignity and not stooping to her level. The most important thing, according to counsellors, is dealing with and overcoming your grief. Smashing her Smurf CDs may not win her back, but it will make you feel a hell of a lot better – and you'd be doing the music business a favour into the bargain.

However, wanton destruction is really only for extreme cases – like being dumped on your birthday, or on the same day that your team has lost at home, or in favour of your father – so generally we would recommend something a shade more subtle. Therefore, if your girlfriend has moved out, but hasn't had time to collect all her belongings, here are a few suggestions:

- Don't fall into the girlie trap of taking a pair of scissors to clothes, simply give her favourite items to Oxfam. After all, she was always banging on about the starving millions.

- Hang one of her bras on the clothes line, fill it with suet and see if the blue tits show any more interest in the contents than you did over the past few months.

- Play frisbee with her CDs.

- Use her all-time favourite Peter Andre CD as a coaster.

- Use her expensive spray cologne to freshen up the loo.

- Empty her bottle of perfume down the loo and replace it with the vinegar from a jar of pickled onions.

- Piss in her bottle of French perfume. The next time she dabs it behind her ears, she'll be reminded of you.

The air to adopt is bitter rather than hurt. You want to convey the impression that the only reason you're angry is on account of the sudden way the relationship ended, not that you're aching in any way. Let her know there are plenty more fish in the sea, even if your rod is a bit rusty.

So on any occasion where you're likely to bump into your ex, make sure you've got a girl on your arm, although draw the line at anyone who is obviously your granny. As far as she who jilted you is concerned, you're having the time of your life. So don't let her catch you hanging around singles' bars or indulging in any of the other activities that give away the fact that you're *sans totty*. These include:

- Getting through more toilet paper than usual.

- Buying dinners for one.

- Enrolling in art evening classes because it's the only way you'll get to see a naked woman.

- Wearing gallons of aftershave, loud shirts and underpants with a saucy motif.

- Getting turned on by two warthogs mating on *Life On Earth.*

- Always being available for drinks after work.

- Moaning about Christmas.

- Fancying anyone called Beryl.

- Taking a keen interest in the *Time Out* classifieds.

- Chatting up the traffic warden who has just arranged for your car to be towed away.

If you do come across your ex with her new bloke, seize the opportunity with both hands, much as you used to do with her buttocks.

9 THINGS TO SAY TO YOUR EX-GIRLFRIEND IN FRONT OF HER NEW BLOKE

1. 'Nice to see you again, Sally... oh, sorry, Laura.'
2. 'You shouldn't have let yourself go like you have – all good things come to an end some time.'
3. 'Me? I'm seeing an actress.' (She doesn't have to know it's only on celluloid).
4. 'Thanks for your farewell present. The rash has gone now.'

5. 'Do they still call you the Irish Open?'

6. 'I see you've lowered your standards.'

7. 'So you've found another mug.'

8. 'I've still got your Bob Monkhouse posters if you want them.'

9. 'You'll never guess who I met the other week? Somebody who hadn't slept with you...'

And if you learn that your ex-girlfriend is getting married, what better wedding gift to send than table mats? But instead of Cotswold scenes or the flora of Britain, dig out an old photo of the pair of you with your tongues down each other's throats and have that made into a nice set of dinner mats.

Chapter Four:

Bits and Pieces

Behaving Badly Accessories

Bag of Laughs

As the name implies, this has nothing to do with Freddie Starr, but is a contraption which lets out a raucous 'Ho, ho, ho' when you squeeze it. The most obvious places to use it are in the pub, in the office or at dinner parties when someone cracks a distinctly unfunny joke, but its element of surprise and mocking laughter can be just as effective in more unusual situations, such as...

- At the height of lovemaking, just as your partner is about to reach orgasm.

- As your boss clears his desk, having been sacked for financial and sexual irregularities.

- Just as they lower your boss's coffin into the ground.

- When Paul Ince gets sent off.

- When your dad is lecturing you about your irresponsible behaviour and how you won't take anything seriously.

- When your girlfriend is lecturing you about the situation in Central America.

- In a library.

- When your mother-in-law slips over on an icy pavement.

- At the World Snooker Championships when Stephen Hendry misses an easy pink.

- When your girlfriend discovers you have substituted Copydex for the toothpaste.

- During the Royal Shakespeare Company production of *King Lear*.

- When your mate realizes that the blind date you'd set him up with was his own mother.

- When your mate finds that you've stitched up the ends of his shirt sleeves.

- When Michael Schumacher retires during the British Grand Prix.

- When Rodney in the marketing department discovers that you've stuck 'Wanker' to the back of his jacket.

- In the audience at *Question Time*.

- While listening to a Leonard Cohen album.

Baldy Wig

If you want to convince people that you're Michael Stipe out of R.E.M. or that you've recently suffered a nasty case of alopecia, this is the ideal purchase. And the great thing with this particular form of baldness is that you can just peel it off when you've made your point without having to worry about investing in a toupee which looks as if it's come straight from a craft fair, or an expensive transplant which leaves your head looking like a badly plucked turkey. Let's face it, if Elton John's money can't buy a snigger-free cure, what hope is there for the rest of us? The baldy wig is best used with people you haven't seen for some time. For example, if you're at university and are going home for the summer holidays, give your parents the shock of their lives by turning up bald. Or wear it to work on a Monday morning saying that you've had such a stressful weekend that all your hair has fallen out and you'll need two weeks' sick leave. If you paint a pink dot on the top of your baldy wig, you can also join in lesbian love sessions by posing as a fifth tit. However, the baldy wig is a bit of a waste of money if you're bald anyway.

Chest Wig

Once upon a time a hairy chest was seen as a sign of virility. Tarzan wouldn't have been half as successful with chicks if he'd only had two wiry little tufts sprouting from his upper torso. Attitudes now though, have turned full circle. Women of today don't want masses of bodily hair on their men, with the result that people like Richard Keys are seen as first cousin to the Wild Man of Borneo. Nevertheless, a chest wig can raise a titter when you strip off for the first time with a new girlfriend. Make sure your relationship's already on a reasonably sound footing before you try it, though, or you might not see her for dust. The joke can also fall a trifle flat if she turns out to have an even hairier body.

Eyes on Stalks

An old favourite – the pair of glasses with eyes which bulge out on coiled stalks. Ideal for shocking the life out of aged relatives and for showing your appreciation of a real babe, these can be worn with confidence at parties, at work or at college. But beware: the novelty can wear off after you've done it for the sixth time, at which point you are more likely to get a finger in your real eye. Since they impair your vision, it is probably not a good idea to wear them while driving in the fast lane on the M6, nor should they be worn in the presence of the family of the late Marty Feldman.

Fake Blood Capsules

Boundless fun can be had with these simple capsules which you slip in your mouth and then bite to allow rivers of blood to flow down your face. As with all practical jokes, timing is everything. For instance, during sex is probably not a good time.

12 SITUATIONS FOR USING FAKE BLOOD CAPSULES

1. In hospital, just as the doctor is doing his rounds.
2. Over Christmas lunch, seconds after you've complained that you've swallowed the coin in the Christmas pudding.
3. At an interview for a job you don't really want.
4. At a dinner party, moments after you've said you thought there was a piece of glass in the trout meunière.

5. To escape from a particularly dull evening with neighbours, just as the slides of Majorca are being loaded.

6. In a doctor's waiting room, to get seen first.

7. If you want to get into town near the hospital, but haven't got enough for the bus fare.

8. During your wedding vows, if you get cold feet at the last minute or just to see the look on the vicar's face.

9. When you fancy a week off work.

10. When the girl you fancy looks like copping off with your best mate.

11. When Jehovah's Witnesses come to call.

12. Any time when you're not getting enough attention.

Fake Dog Mess

Plastic dog poos come specially moulded, either with the imprint of a size-ten shoe or to fit snugly around your footwear. As such, they are ideal for bringing into somebody else's house after a walk in the park. Even though they are odourless, you can guarantee that the woman of the house will complain about the foul smell the moment she spots what you've dragged in. The effect may be short-lived, but it is nonetheless worthwhile especially if you follow this list of doggy dos and don'ts:

Do

- Apologize profusely for bringing the mess on to her new carpet.

- Pretend that you too can smell it.

- Taste it and confirm, 'Yes, it's definitely a dog turd. At a guess, I'd say Red Setter.'

Don't

- Over-act, or she'll smell a rat... well a rat with the trots.

Fake Willy

It's pink, it's wrinkly and it hangs out your trousers. No, it's not your mum – it's a fake willy. Alarmingly realistic, the fake willy can be employed as a shock tactic on any manner of unsuspecting victims – the vicar, your mother-in-law, the Round Table collecting for Christmas, basically anyone you're not trying to impress. Be careful where you use it in public, however. Avoid wearing it under a grubby mac, around men's toilets or anywhere too close to a police station. Nor is it a sensible tool to use to try and chat up a girl. Even if she doesn't think you're some kind of pervert, she may end up preferring it to the real thing.

False Nose

Wearing a large false nose can be a hoot at any party – unless, of course, it takes half an hour before anybody notices that you look any different. Cheaper and less permanent than plastic surgery, a false nose can transform your personality. It may even make you a hit with women. Sporting an elephant's trunk, you can casually remark – in that cool yet confident way of yours – that the trunk isn't the only thing about your person of which an elephant might be proud. Naturally, however, she will be disappointed if it's your ears.

When wearing a false nose at a party, you must also take into account your extra inches. The joke will wear a shade thin if you knock over a tray of drinks every time you turn round or poke somebody's eye out with your beak.

Places Not to Ware a False Nose

- At a meeting of the Barry Manilow Appreciation Society.

- In the toucan house at London Zoo.

- During a passionate snog.

- On the Underground in rush hour.

- On your wedding photos.

- On anybody else's wedding photos.

- On your passport photo.

- On the photo to accompany your application form to become a male model.

- On the photo to accompany your application form to join a dating agency.

- In a crowded lift.

- When you've got a heavy cold.

False Teeth

A set of false teeth can make or break a new relationship at a party. By manipulating your gums, saying 'Sorry, these new teeth are killing me' and whipping out a pair of dentures, you will either impress her with your wacky sense of humour or send her screaming hysterically from the room. Therefore before attempting the manoeuvre, it is worth spending a few moments to gauge into which category she is likely to fall.

False teeth are also extremely good value around the elderly, the infirm or the plain stupid. If granny keeps her dentures in a glass in the bathroom, swap hers for your fake set and watch her struggle to speak coherently. Your parents will probably decide she's drunk again and have her put in a home. You could try wearing false teeth on your next visit to the dentist, but remember, unless your dentist sees the funny side – and dentists aren't noted for their sense of mirth – he will exact a full and painful revenge with the vast array of sharp implements at his disposal. Is any joke worth not being able to talk for three days? A better idea is to put your false teeth in unexpected places, such as:

- Down the side of the sofa when your mum's dusting.

- Inside a cream sponge or a trifle.

- On the seat of grandad's favourite armchair.

- In the goldfish bowl.

- On someone's coffin.

- In your mum's slippers.

- In the secretary's top drawer at the office.

- On your tutor's desk at college.

- In the hood of a work colleague's anorak.

- In the pocket of your boss's coat.

• If possible, in the bowl where the FA Cup draw is made.

You can also buy rotting teeth – brown, crumbly and positively revolting and therefore a sure way of gaining entry to the local British Legion. They also come in handy for scaring walkers in churchyards at dusk, but are definitely not recommended to be worn at an audition for a toothpaste commercial.

False Tits

False tits are to subtlety what Kenneth Williams was to Rugby League. They're big, brash and in your face and, as such, are the perfect accessory to be worn on stuffy occasions such as a Buckingham Palace garden party or in the enclosure at Royal Ascot. And on stag nights, they go down better than Linda Lovelace. You can even get your mates to sign them. However, it has to be said that they won't cut much ice with your girlfriend, particularly since they're almost certain to be bigger than hers, and in any case you should only wear them sparingly. If you find yourself wanting to wear them every day, it may be time to see a shrink.

Fart Spray

A handy spray which captures the essence of your lounge half an hour after a hearty portion of Brussels sprouts. It comes in a choice of other flavours too, including baked bean, curry, cabbage, steak and onion and her husband arriving home unexpectedly early. Laced with glorious hydrogen sulphide – the 'bad eggs' gas which every schoolboy tries to produce in science lessons – the spray is ideal for getting rid of unwanted callers. Still, always remember to follow the dosage levels on the can:

- Nosy neighbour, one squirt.

- Double-glazing salesman, two squirts.

- Mother-in-law, two squirts.

- Mother-in-law with a heavy cold, three squirts.

- Mother-in-law with a heavy cold and a bone to pick, four squirts.

- Jehovah's Witnesses, the whole can.

Used with discretion, fart spray can be invaluable in securing a seat on a crowded bus or the London Underground. Even the most militant pensioner will be forced to flee their specially designated seat in the face of a full onslaught. It is also beneficial in other confined spaces such as packed lifts, although it is not recommended for use during an attempt to break the world record for the number of students able to cram themselves into a phone-box. The spray could also be turned to your advantage at an important business meeting – you could suddenly find yourself heading for unexpected promotion by blaming the smell on Simpkins from the Basildon office. Unlikely as it may seem, the spray could also be of assistance in affairs of the heart. If you and your mate are chatting up the same girl at a club, simply squirt the spray behind his buttocks and get in first with the blame for the stink. She'll immediately opt for you in preference to someone whose marriage vows may have to include a reference to trapped wind. The only side effect to the spray is that it may make you irresistible to dogs.

Inflatable Doll

An inflatable doll can be your best friend – indeed sometimes your only friend. As such, every single bloke should own one although you'll need to pass it off as a novelty lilo when your mum comes to visit. As can be seen from the list below, the advantages of a blow-up woman greatly outweigh those of the real thing.

Advantages of an Inflatable Woman

- She's always smiling.

- She doesn't nag.

- She never has headaches.

- She doesn't have a mother.

- She can cope with anything except sharp objects.

- She's a cheap date.

- She doesn't spend hours in the bathroom washing her hair.

- She's never too tired.

- She doesn't get pregnant.

- She'll do it anywhere you like.

- She doesn't need any foreplay.

- She doesn't get rat-arsed and make a show of herself in public.

- She doesn't suffer from advanced acne.

- She doesn't cost you a fortune in clothes.

- She doesn't consider premature ejaculation to be a problem.

- You can share her with your mates without her thinking you're some kind of weirdo.

Disadvantages of an Inflatable Woman

- She tends to go down on you, but not on the way you want.

- She can't cook.

- She can develop alarming wrinkles if she gets too close to the fire.

- Her conversation is limited.

- The noises she makes during sex can be off-putting.

- She can't drive you to the pub.

- If she goes on top outdoors on a windy day, there is a danger that you might never see her again.

Lunch Box

Sticking a cucumber or a large carrot down the front of your trousers is an old ploy for pulling chicks. However, it only works with certain types of girls and probably won't impress a lady magistrate, the chairperson of the local townswomen's guild, the barmaid at a lesbian pub, your granny, a seaside landlady, a nun, delegates to a conference on feminism or anyone who is in labour. It can also be something of a disappointment to the girl in question when you fail to live up to expectations, but consolation may be at hand if she turns out to have a fetish about vegetables.

Maggot Slime

Placed on a saucer, this gooey, greenish gunge, liberally sprinkled with realistic-looking maggots, is the perfect way to stop your family raiding the fridge. It can also be brought into play at dinner parties, office functions, wedding receptions, family Christmas lunches and in posh restaurants where you might be able to obtain a refund while the distraught chef, all too aware of the impending loss of two stars, hacks himself to death with his meat cleaver. However, maggot slime won't create much of a stir in student accommodation where it will simply be considered par for the (first) course.

Plastic Spider

OK, so we all know plastic spiders look nothing like the real thing and are about as convincing as Dick Van Dyke's Cockney accent in *Mary Poppins*, but they can still be pretty unnerving to arachnaphobes. Basically, such people are scared of anything with eight legs, which means they'd probably be equally terrified by the Liverpool midfield or if confronted by half of the Home Counties (South) formation dancing team.

Plastic spiders are particularly good value for putting in beds, lunch-boxes (the sort that actually contain sandwiches) and on your mum's shoulder when she wakes up from a long sleep.

Stick-on Scar

Some girls go for dangerous-looking men, which probably explains why Dale Winton probably hasn't got a girlfriend at present. They are swept along by the excitement, the adrenaline rush of living close to the edge and then they go running to their mum when the Mr Mean and Macho dumps them three weeks later for their best friend Mandy. So if you're looking for a permanent relationship, a stick-on scar on your face is probably not a good idea as sooner or later you'll have to remove it and she'll discover that you look more like Charles Hawtrey than Charles Bronson. For a one-night stand, though, a fake scar can possess considerable pulling power, provided you don't do any of the following when wearing it:

- Wear anything pink.

- Order a Babycham, despite what the adverts say.

- Say you've got to be in by ten o'clock because your mum gets worried.

- Dance to the latest 911 single.

- Complain that loud music always bring on one of your funny turns.

- Bring your knitting.

- Carry a pouch purse.

- Wear your scar in a pub or club where all the other blokes have got bigger scars – and real ones at that.

Viking Helmet

Ideal for looting, pillaging and hanging spare coats on, a plastic Viking helmet will show everyone that you're not a guy to be messed with. Conjuring up images of power, passion and depravity, it is therefore the ideal accessory for the office party where you will be able to answer in spades the inevitable question of whether or not you're feeling horny. It is, however, less advisable to wear a Viking helmet during a serious proposal of marriage (unless your girlfriend is Norwegian), during a job interview (unless it's for Scandinavian Seaways) or in the vicinity of a bull. And whilst it is very tempting to keep it on during sex, it is worth remembering that it does make you look a complete prat.

8 THINGS YOU SHOULD NOT ATTEMPT WITH A PLASTIC HELMET

1. Clean the car with it.
2. Mate with it.
3. Attach wheels to it and ride it on the M25.
4. Use it to perform a do-it-yourself enema.
5. Use it as a saucepan.
6. Play frisbee with it.
7. Sail across the Atlantic in it.
8. Pretend it's the FA Cup.

Whoopee Cushion

Show us someone who doesn't laugh at the sound of a whoopee cushion and we'll show you Robert Killjoy-Sulk. This perennial weapon of merry-making is guaranteed to crack up even the stoniest face and frankly anybody who refuses to join in the fun should be rounded up and lynched from the nearest tree. If you can't find a tree, a telegraph pole will just about do, but remember to get permission from BT first. The key element to the success of a whoopee-cushion prank is surprise, so make sure you put it in the last place anybody would expect. This might include:

- On a High Court judge's seat as he is about to begin the afternoon session.

- On your boss's seat when he is about to deliver a severe reprimand about the standard of your work.

- In the Royal box at Wembley.

- On the Speaker's chair in the House of Commons.

- On your driving examiner's seat.

- On your bank manager's chair as he is about to consider the matter of your overdraft.

- On the organist's seat when he is about to play the first hymn at a funeral service.

- On the sofa as the vicar is about to sit down and take afternoon tea at your parents' house.

- On the custody sergeant's chair as he is about to caution for you being drunk in charge of an inflatable ostrich.

- In your mate's bed as he is about to score with his new girlfriend.

- On your psychiatrist's chair as he attempts to analyse the reasons for your juvenile behaviour.

- Under your wife while she is in the process of giving birth.